THE MANAGER'S POCKET GUIDE TO TEAM SPONSORSHIP

By Sara Pope
Cornelius and Associates

HRD PRESS
Amherst, Massachusetts

&

Lakewood Publications
Minneapolis, Minnesota

Published by:
HRD Press
22 Amherst Road
Amherst, MA 01002
1-800-822-2801
   (U.S. and Canada)
1-413-253-3488
1-413-253-3490 (Fax)
http://www.hrdpress.com

Lakewood Publications
50 South Ninth Street
Minneapolis, MN 55402
1-800-707-7769
1-612-340-4819 (Fax)
http://www.trainingsupersite.com

ISBN 0-87425-421-3

Production services by Clark Riley
Cover design by Eileen Klockars
Editorial services by Mary George
Illustrations by Eileen Blyth

 PRINTED IN CANADA

TABLE OF CONTENTS

About the Author

WELCOME TO THE WORLD OF TEAM SPONSORSHIP!

This compact, easy-to-use guide is designed to help you understand your role as a team sponsor and to ensure your success in carrying out that role. It covers the steps that every sponsor must take to see that a team gets started on the right track, continues in the right direction, and adds value to the business. As you work through this guide, you will find terms, definitions, checklists, and exercises.

At the end, you will find the Team Sponsor Test, which will help you identify any areas or issues you need to review before sponsoring a team.

THE FOUR TEAM-SUPPORT ELEMENTS

There are certain elements that must be in place to support the growth and development of teams. As the sponsor of a team, you are one of those necessary elements. However, you alone are not enough. All together, there are four elements:

1. **An identified sponsor**
2. **A clear purpose**
3. **The means to measure accomplishments**
4. **The resources and time to work toward the clear purpose**

Since you are the first of these four elements, we know that your team has this base covered. Now your job is to ensure that the other three are in place.

☞ **Remember. . .**

No matter what type of team you are sponsoring, all four team-support elements must be in place.

This guide will focus on three specific types of teams: ad hoc, standing, and natural.

Now before we get into the hands-on skills for each type of team, let's review our key terminology, the definitions of the team types, and the roles that support teams.

KEY TERMS AND DEFINITIONS

Throughout this guide, we will use the following words a lot, so let's make sure we are all speaking the same language.

TERM	DEFINITION	TYPE OF TEAM
MISSION STATEMENT	This is the broad business purpose for which a team has been formed. Mission statements are usually brief, formal statements that show the direction or purpose of the team. They are a kind of "creed" that the team lives by. The mission statement should be accepted by all the team members.	• Standing • Natural
GOALS	A team's goals are the specific, measurable aims or ends at which the team's efforts are directed.	• Ad hoc • Standing • Natural
OBJECTIVES	Something at which effort is directed; an aim or end of action; a position to be attained or purpose to be achieved. We will use this term interchangeably with **goal**.	• Ad hoc • Standing • Natural
METRICS	These are the measures that teams develop in order to gauge their success.	• Ad hoc • Standing • Natural

THE THREE TYPES OF TEAMS

The three types of teams that we will address in this guide, and their definitions and purpose, are presented below.

TEAM	DEFINITION	PURPOSE
AD HOC	A group of people working together toward a specific business goal or objective. The team may consist of functional or cross-functional membership. Members usually serve on the team in addition to their normal job duties. It is a temporary team that **always** disbands once the goal (or set of goals) has been reached.	To solve a specific problem or resolve a specific issue
STANDING	A group of people who meet periodically to work on a recurring or critical business purpose or issue. This is usually a team that does not disband because of the nature of the issue (safety, quality, etc.). Standing team membership is normally shifted according to a set of rotational rules, and members ordinarily serve in addition to their regular duties.	To plan for, strategize, and deal with long-term recurring or critical issues
NATURAL	A group of people completing interdependent tasks, or working on common products, customers, or purposes. A natural team is an intact work group that may be constructed functionally (e.g., the human resource department) or cross-functionally (e.g., a process team, a product team, or a work cell).	To carry out the daily work efficiently and cost-effectively. To push decision making closer to actual work

THE ROLES THAT SUPPORT TEAMS

Now we come to the last part of our review—the roles that must be in place to support teams.

ROLE	FUNCTION
SPONSOR	The sponsor is the person who is responsible for starting or "chartering" the team. The sponsor removes roadblocks, provides resources, and gets help for the team when needed.
	The sponsor is not a member of the team and only occasionally attends meetings. However, the sponsor **does** intervene if he or she believes that the team has gotten off track or is working on goals that are inconsistent with its original mission. The team sponsor **does not** micro-manage, steer the team toward a particular outcome, or dictate solutions to the team.
LEADER	The team leader is an administrative coordinator for the team. The leader ensures that the team is using good team processes, ensures that all team members are involved, and coordinates the efforts of all the team members.
	The team leader **is not** a mini-supervisor, **is not** any more accountable for the success of the team than any other team member, and **is not** "in charge" of the team.

THE ROLES THAT SUPPORT TEAMS (Concluded)

ROLE	FUNCTION
MEMBERS	The team members are members of the team because of their particular area of responsibility (natural) or expertise (ad hoc or standing). Team members are responsible for the success of the team's efforts and thus must come to the team with a mind-set of working together toward a common goal, a commitment to consensus, and an attitude that the input of all members is critical.
FACILITATOR	This role helps to guide the team in using good team processes. The facilitator is a group dynamics expert who ensures the team is using the brainpower and input of all team members by following good group processes and problem solving.
TEAMS COORDINATOR	This is the person who monitors the development of teams in your facility. The coordinator's job is to make sure that projects are not being duplicated and that teams are working on issues that fit into the facility's priorities. This person may also coordinate assignment of facilitators.

Now that we're through discussing terminology, let's take a look at your "formal" job description as a team sponsor.

TEAM SPONSOR

Job Summary

The sponsor is the management person who is responsible for officially starting (or "chartering") a particular ad hoc team, natural team, or standing team. The sponsor provides resources, removes roadblocks, and acts as the management "champion" for the efforts of the team. The sponsor also determines when to disband the team.

Principal Duties

1. Determines the need to officially "sanction" the creation of an ad hoc team, natural team, or standing team to accomplish a business purpose.

2. Provides guidance, ensures that the team has clear direction, and either writes the team's "charter" or approves it.

3. Provides (or allocates) organizational resources needed for the team to accomplish its goals.

4. Actively monitors the performance of the team against its goals by reviewing team minutes, holding periodic meetings with the team leader, and occasionally attending team meetings.

5. Determines when to formally disband the team, either because the team has accomplished its goals or because the team is unable to accomplish its goals.

6. If the team is multi-disciplinary and cross-functional (i.e., team members have supervisors other than the team sponsor), the sponsor works with relevant other management personnel to ensure that the team members have the time to work on team goals. Also, the sponsor works to resolve conflicting demands that are made on team members by other management personnel.

7. Represents the interests of the team in discussions with upper management and other management personnel in the organization.

8. Responds to requests for help from the team, provides encouragement, and works to remove barriers to team success.

9. Ensures that team successes are documented and publicized.

Requirements

The team sponsor must be high enough in the management hierarchy to provide or acquire the resources needed by the team to accomplish its goals. The sponsor must have. . .

- An extremely good understanding of, and familiarity with, the key management personalities in the facility

- A good understanding of how to bring about change in the organization

- The ability to influence others, particularly upper management

The team sponsor role may seem daunting, and it is a pretty tough role to fill. The sponsor is in the difficult position of determining where the organization's resources will be allocated and which employees should be involved, and then evaluating and measuring successes. All these functions have a precedent in traditional management; in fact, traditional managers had the same list of responsibilities, as well as the task of deciding the "how to's." The major difference between the sponsor and the traditional manager is that the manager usually had to determine what was to be done, how to do it, and who would do it. The sponsor still has the major responsibility of deciding what has to be done—then the team takes over the "how to's."

| **Traditional Managers** | ➤ What to do |
| | ➤ How to do it |

| **Team Sponsor** | ➤ What to do |
| **Team** | ➤ How to do it |

Now that we have a common understanding of the general terms, definitions, roles, and responsibilities related to team sponsorship, we're ready to take a closer look at the different types of teams. Each of these teams—ad hoc, standing, and natural—has its own unique foundation. Your first task as sponsor is to ensure that the team has a strong foundation in place before it begins.

In Chapter 1, we will cover your specific responsibilities for an **ad hoc team**. Chapter 2 will instruct you on the specifics for sponsoring a **standing team**. And finally, in Chapter 3, we will cover **natural teams**.

CHAPTER 1
SPONSORING AN AD HOC TEAM

 The first type of team we'll consider is ad hoc teams. Begin by asking yourself the following three key questions and give honest answers regarding the project you are considering sponsoring.

QUESTION	Yes	No	I Don't Know
1. Does it really take a team of people to solve this problem?	❏	❏	❏
2. Am I sure that I haven't already made up my mind **how** I want this problem solved?	❏	❏	❏
3. If this is going to take a lot of money or resources to fix, am I sure that it fits into the facility's priorities? That is, can I justify it?	❏	❏	❏

Only if you can honestly answer all three questions with a resounding, unreserved "yes" should you read on. If you responded "no" to any of them, then STOP, go back! You are not ready to form a team. If you answered "I don't know" to any question, then you must do some research and information gathering to find out the answer.

Suppose you're ready to form your team. What next? The following checklist and step-by-step guide gives you a fail-proof method for sponsoring an ad hoc team.

11

SPONSOR'S CHECKLIST FOR AD HOC TEAMS

Task to Be Completed	✓ Check when Complete
1. Write first draft of goal statement.	❏
2. Determine time frame, boundaries, and budget.	❏
3. Go to the teams coordinator and have a facilitator assigned.	❏
4. Review charter with facilitator; finalize.	❏
5. Appoint the team leader.	❏
6. Meet with team leader to determine membership.	❏
7. Ensure that there is a meeting with each team member to discuss the project and gain their commitment to it.	❏
8. Meet with each team member's supervisor to ensure commitment to the project.	❏
9. Complete the charter form.	❏
10. Get input from the team and finalize the charter. Ensure that all team members:	❏
• understand the goal statement	❏
• understand the boundaries	❏
• understand the budget and resources	❏
11. Ensure that the team develops appropriate metrics.	❏
12. Actively monitor the team's progress throughout the course of the project.	❏
13. Intervene when needed or when asked.	❏
14. Publicize the team's results.	❏
15. Disband the team.	❏

Step 1

Step 1: Write the first draft of the goal statement.

You have probably had it drummed into your head that every team has to have a charter. Here we will beat that drum one more time. **EVERY Team Must Have A Charter**! Before going any further, turn to Appendix A and study the completed charter for ad hoc teams. Notice that it includes the following:

1. The specific goal or problem to be solved
2. The time frame in which it is to be completed
3. The boundaries
4. The budget and other available resources

Let's take a closer look at the first item above, because drafting the goal statement is your first task as a sponsor. (The other three items will be discussed in the section "Step 2.")

Specific goals will result in clear expectations. Compare these examples:

GENERAL	↔	SPECIFIC
Set up more lines	↔	Set up three new lines
Set up new lines as soon as possible	↔	Set up three new lines this year
Do it cost effectively	↔	Limit spending to $100,000

It is easy to see that adding specifics to the goal provides clarity. Given a well-defined goal—such as setting up three new lines within one year for $100,000—a team can understand exactly what it will take to be successful. But given a poorly defined goal, there is lots of room for interpretation.

Your job in writing the charter is to minimize the need for interpretation.

Stating the expected outcomes is one way to make the goal more specific. Outcomes can be stated in three basic ways:

1. **Physical Units**—quantity of production, market share, number of errors
2. **Time**—meeting deadlines, servicing customers, completing a project
3. **Money**—profits, sales, budgets

You should tell the team specifically what outcomes you are looking for. You can state the expected outcomes in several different ways. For example:

- 65,000 widgets produced
- Delivery of 65,000 widgets by June 19
- $65,000 worth of widgets sold

Here is a step-by-step process to help you write a goal statement that is clear, specific, and motivating.

Step A Goal Statement	Write down the objective or task that you would like the team to accomplish. Do you want them to reduce costs? Increase sales? Enhance quality? Improve customer service?

Step B Expected Outcomes	Specify the standard or target to be reached. For example, produce sixty units per hour, attain a 10% lower reject rate, answer all customer inquiries within 24 hours.

It's time to try some exercises so that you will get the hang of this process before you start working on the real thing.

Practice Exercise — Three Cases

Case 1

You are responsible for a group of mechanics charged with installing new machinery. This installation will take down the lines for at least one full day and possibly two. You have talked with the production manager, and he says that the best time to do the job is at the beginning of next week; however, things must be fully operational by the end of the shift on Wednesday. The new equipment must be tested for at least 24 hours to ensure that it is operating properly.

---

 1. Write down the objective or task that you would like the team to accomplish.

 2. Specify the expected outcomes.

Case 2

You have a team of accounting assistants reporting to you. Your company has just purchased another plant, and its employees must be converted to your payroll system by the end of January. It is now January 4. All necessary paperwork must be completed in time to run a test of the system a couple of days before payday, February 1. You are forming an ad hoc team of the four accounting assistants, along with the plant's personnel officer, to accomplish this task.

---

 1. Write down the objective or task that you would like the team to accomplish.

(Continued)

Practice Exercise — Three Cases *(Concluded)*

   2. Specify the expected outcomes.

Case 3

The production group reporting to you is working on some brand-new equipment. You have noticed that since the equipment was installed, the group's reject rate has been going up. Rejects due to scratched widgets have increased to 23%, up from 11%. Although scratched widgets can be sold, they must be sold at a reduced price. You want the group to get the rate back to at least where it was before the new equipment was installed.

   1. Write down the objective or task that you would like the team to accomplish.

   2. Specify the expected outcomes.

Now compare your work to the sample answers given in Appendix B. The samples show how expert sponsors would have responded.

Exercise — Drafting the Goal Statement

Using the two-step process, write your first draft.

Step A Goal Statement	Write down the objective or task that you would like the team to accomplish. Do you want them to reduce costs? Increase sales? Enhance quality? Improve customer service?

Step B Expected Outcomes	Specify the standard or target to be reached. For example, produce sixty units per hour, attain a 10% lower reject rate, answer all customer inquiries within 24 hours.

The objective or task that I would like my team to accomplish is. . .

_____

_____

_____

The specific outcomes I expect are. . .

_____

_____

_____

_____

Step 2

Step 2: Determine the time frame, boundaries, and budget.

Time Frames

The time frame in which the project is to be completed is simply a judgment call. Ad hoc teams should be working on projects that can be completed within six months. During the commitment to the charter phase, you should get some input from the team members about whether the time frame you have suggested is reasonable and realistic.

Boundaries

The boundaries are the things that the team **can** do and **cannot** do. By setting limits at the beginning, you are letting team members know the rules of the game before they start playing. No one wants to have the rules made up along the way, and too often that is what happens with teams. Take a look at the examples below.

The team **can**
- ask for bids or quotes from vendors
- make a formal recommendation
- make the decision and implement it
- move existing equipment

The team **cannot**
- purchase any new equipment
- conduct trials in a manner that affects production on other lines
- make changes that have an impact on internal customers without getting their "buy-in"
- make a commitment to a vendor or supplier

Budget and Other Resources

The budget and resources area affords the
sponsor an opportunity to be creative. We
tend to think of resources as simply dollars
and cents. However, there are other ways that
sponsors can provide their teams with
resources. At times, simply naming someone
who is the team's assigned expert is a resource
to the team. Here are a few examples of
resources that are not necessarily budget items:

- Visits to vendors, suppliers, or other plants
- Allowing meetings on overtime
- Ensuring that team members know whom they may
  invite to their meetings (managers, supervisors,
  technical experts, or even their sponsor)

If the team does have a budget, it is important to ensure that
they know procedures for spending that money. If none of the
members have had experience with the purchasing department
or with the purchasing practices of your organization, assign a
specific person in the purchasing department as their resource.
For hourly production teams, this is particularly important, as
they generally have had little experience with organizational
purchasing.

Step 3 Step 3: Go to the teams coordinator and
have a facilitator assigned.

The facilitator will be a critical
factor in helping the team
through the project. It just
makes good sense to have this
person involved early on in the
project, so that the facilitator
and team members can develop
the partnership necessary for
success.

Step 4: Review the draft charter with the facilitator and finalize.

Even though we've given you step-by-step instructions and practice exercises, you don't have to go it alone. Take the draft charter to the facilitator and get suggestions for improvements or revisions.

 Step 5: Appoint the team leader.

There are several factors to consider in appointing the team leader:

➤ It should be someone who has a real interest in solving the problem.
➤ It should be someone who is affected by the problem or issue.
➤ It should be someone who is respected by peers and can lead a team without "taking over."
➤ It should be someone who has the time to devote to the project.

Once you have chosen the team leader, you should sit down together and determine the rest of the membership. You may want to enlist the facilitator's help with this task as well.

By the way, the last factor may be the most critical. It won't matter how interested the person is in solving the problem if he or she doesn't have the time to work on the team. Make sure that the person you have selected is not serving on more than one other team and will have time needed to lead your team to success.

Sometimes the team decides who the team leader will be. Usually this only occurs when the team has plenty of time to solve their problem and when the team members have had some experience with serving on teams. If you would like the team to determine the team leader, simply skip this step and go straight to step six.

Step 6 Step 6: Meet with the team leader to determine membership.

Like the leader, team members should be chosen because they have a real interest in solving the problem. Take into consideration each team member's. . .

➤ Aptitude for solving the problem
➤ Motivation to solve the problem
➤ Experience with the problem
➤ Time available to work on the problem

The team members may be internal suppliers or internal customers of the problem area. It may make their lives easier or better to have this problem solved. Try to put together a group of diverse thinkers. If everyone has the same point of view as yourself or the team leader, you might as well have solved the problem by yourself.

Step 7 Step 7: Ensure that there is a meeting with each team member to discuss the project and gain their commitment to it.

This is a lot of time that we're asking of you, isn't it? All this meeting and ensuring is probably beginning to wear you out. Well, notice that with this step you only have to make sure that someone meets with each team member. If you do not have the time, the team leader may be able to hold these meetings. Another approach is for you and the team leader to split the list.

In these meetings, the team member has a chance to ask any questions about the project, and you can determine whether this person is truly interested in solving the problem at hand. If someone simply does not want to serve on the team, or does not feel that he or she has the time for it, do not force the issue! Remember, a team member's interest in solving the problem is the key to his or her motivation, which is essential.

This is also a good opportunity to find out how many teams the person is already serving on. Keep in mind that we do not want people serving on more than two teams at one time.

Step 8 **Step 8: Meet individually with the supervisor of each team member to ensure commitment to the project.**

This step is only necessary when sponsoring a cross-functional team. Obviously, if the team members all report to you, you know your level of commitment—it's pretty high or you would not have read this far. However, if you are asking people from other areas to work on a project, you need to ensure that their supervisors will give them the time and the latitude to do so.

If the team will take a lot of time or effort, ask the supervisor if any other projects or tasks could be put on hold. Often the people who are the best team players are "rewarded" by having more projects heaped on them. Take this chance to see whether there is any way to lighten the load while members work on your project.

Step 9 **Step 9: Complete the charter form.**

Finally! All this work and now you get to put the charter into final draft form. Note that I said **draft** form. Even at this point, you're not finished; there is still a possibility of revision. Notice the charter form on the next page. Complete the form; then you and the team leader can schedule the team's first meeting.

AD HOC TEAM CHARTER

Goal Statement

_____
_____
_____

Team Sponsor: _____
Team Leader: _____
Assigned Facilitator: _____
Time Frame: _____

Names of Team Members

Boundaries

Budget/Resources

Step 10 — Step 10: Get input from the team and finalize the charter.

To finalize the charter you need to review three factors:

1. The goal statement
2. The boundaries
3. The budget

There are several ways that you can accomplish this:

☞ The sponsor meets with the team and reviews the draft.
☞ The facilitator meets with the team and reviews the draft.
☞ The sponsor presents the draft and then allows the team to meet alone to develop a list of questions. The team members let the sponsor know if they need to meet again.

Regardless of which method you use, ensure that the team has a good understanding of the goal, time frames, and boundaries.

Also, be certain that the team members believe the goal is achievable. You want them to feel challenged, but at the same time, you don't want to set them up for failure. Remember, the purpose of this step is to gain commitment to the charter; you should be willing to compromise if the team members feel strongly about an issue.

If you and the team agree to changes, make sure that the changes are made **in writing**.

It has taken **10** steps just to get to the point where the team can start working. Yet, by taking this time on the front end, you have virtually eliminated any chance of misunderstanding or disagreement about the project. You can be sure that every hour spent on the project from this point forward will be focused on achieving the project's goal.

Congratulations!

You have done your job as sponsor in getting the team started on the right track. Now it's time to step aside and let the team members do the job you've chartered them to do. Of course, you still have to lend them support and keep them on track; but you should never micro-manage. Steps 11 through 15 will give you some suggestions for helping the team without overdoing it.

Step 11 Step 11: Ensure that the team develops appropriate metrics.

One of the first tasks that the team must perform is to develop the metrics planning table. Metrics are simply the **measures** that the team will use. By developing the metrics, the team is determining how they are going to measure and report their performance to you, the sponsor. (See Appendix C for an example of a completed metrics table.)

Your task as sponsor is to evaluate the metrics to guarantee they tell you what you need to know. The following three rules of metric development offer guidelines for this evaluation.

Rule 1: The metrics must follow the goal statement.

Sometimes, depending on the goal statement, the metrics will be very clear. For example, if you chartered a team to reduce the time it takes to return customer inquiries, the metrics would be fairly simple for the team to determine; they would track the time it takes to return customer inquiries. In other cases, the metrics may not be as clear. If you chartered the same team to increase customer satisfaction, the team may need to gather data on what the customer wants before they can decide what they will measure in the metrics planning table.

It is your role to monitor these measures and to ensure that the team is gathering the information you will need to determine the success of the project.

Rule 2: Not every ad hoc team will need to use the metric planning table.

Some projects for ad hoc teams will not lend themselves to developing metrics. For instance, if you were sponsoring a team charged with making a recommendation on software to purchase, the only logical measures of success would be these:

- Did they make the recommendation?
- Did they stay within their time frame?

There is no need to use the metrics planning table to track this team's performance.

Rule 3: The metrics are *not* the data the team needs to solve their problem.

Sometimes sponsors confuse the metrics with the problem-solving process. Some teams do need to gather and analyze data in determining the root cause of the problem or the best solution; but this has nothing to do with metrics. Metrics simply allow you to measure whether the team has met the goal that you set out for it in the charter. If you are getting involved in the data that the team is gathering in solving the problem, **You Are Micro-Managing**!

Let's try a brief exercise to get some practice in evaluating metrics:

Exercise — Evaluating Metrics

Situation A

The training team in a plant has been charged with the following:

Goal Statement:
To develop proficiency in problem-solving techniques in the maintenance department

The team developed the following metric:
Track the number of maintenance team members who complete the eight-hour training in problem-solving techniques by April 15.

 Does the metric follow the goal statement? Why or why not?

Situation B

A natural team working on line 2 has set the following goal for themselves:

Goal Statement:
To reduce the top pad scrap generated on line 2

The team developed the following metric:
Chart the amount of top pad scrap on an hourly basis.

 Does the metric follow the goal statement? Why or why not?

Now compare your work to the sample answers in Appendix B.

Okay. Now that you've had some practice, I'm sure that you won't have any problems with evaluating your team's metrics. Just remember the key question: Will this measure tell you if the team reached the goal you set out for it?

Step 12 Step 12: Actively monitor the progress of the team throughout the project.

There are several methods you can use to monitor the team's progress.

1. Hold periodic meetings with the team leader.

Meeting with the team leader on a periodic basis will be helpful in two ways:

- You will be able to get an "insider's" view of how the team is progressing and what kind of support members need from you.
- You will have the opportunity to provide the team leader with the moral support he or she may need.

Leading a team is a difficult task—kind of like walking a tightrope. The team leader is expected to lead without taking over. These meetings will give you a chance to coach the leader in the skills necessary for success.

2. Meet on a regular basis with the facilitator.

The facilitator will be able to give you an "outsider's" view of the team, as well as an expert view of the group dynamics. If the group is having trouble with decision making or problem-solving steps, the facilitator can give you advice on how you can help or what type of training or resources the team needs.

3. Occasionally attend team meetings.

You should not attend team meetings on a regular basis, because it may send the message that you do not trust the team.

However, if you never show up the team may think that you are uninterested. You have to come up with a happy medium. How often is too often will vary with the time frame of the project and the frequency of meetings. You should **always** let the team know in advance that you plan to attend.

4. Review meeting minutes.

Every team should keep a logbook. It is set up at the start of the project and includes the team's charter, ground rules, and any operating guidelines the team has developed. As members meet and work on the project, they log action minutes, agendas, and parking lot forms in sequential order. (For sample forms, see Appendix C.) This record is valuable for monitoring the progress of the team. By reviewing the minutes, you can immediately see if the team is wandering into areas outside its boundaries. The status column of action minutes will show any issues left unresolved; it will help you identify roadblocks and lend clues on where and how to get involved. Remember to review the logbook on a regular basis.

 Step 13: Intervene when needed or asked.

There may be times when you decide you must intervene, and there may be times when the team, the team leader, or the facilitator asks you to intervene. In either instance, you must keep in mind:

> *The purpose of the intervention is not to maim, blame, or shame anyone; it is to identify problems and come up with actions to address those problems.*

There are many different situations that may call for you to get involved. Here are some examples:

- You review the team minutes and find that the team has spent the last three meetings discussing problems that are unrelated to the charter.

Possible Interventions:

— Call a special meeting to review and clarify the charter.
— Meet with the team leader to review the charter.

• You see in the status column of the minutes that any action requiring help from the engineering department remains incomplete.

Possible Interventions:

— Suggest that the team invite the engineering director to their next meeting.
— Meet with the team leader to find out more about the problem.
— Go to the engineering director and see if there is any way to get more engineering time devoted to the project.

• Team members ask you to get involved because they can't get any time in the lab to run their trials. Whenever they try to get time, the equipment is in use.

Possible Interventions:

— Suggest that the team invite the lab supervisor to their next meeting.
— Suggest that the team appoint a member to try to get on the agenda of the next lab team meeting in order to work out an arrangement.
— Go to the lab supervisor and work out an arrangement for the team to use the equipment during an off-shift hour.

These are just a few ways that you can provide support and intervene on behalf of the team. Don't forget, your job is to remove the roadblocks to their success.

Step 14

Step 14: Publicize the team's results.

Once team members have implemented their solution or have made their recommendation, you need to recognize their achievement. This is important for several reasons: first, they have made you look good, and you owe them some public praise; second, it helps team members understand why their efforts were worthwhile and makes them more likely to want to work on future teams and projects; and third, other departments and areas need to know how this problem was solved because the solution may have an impact on them or give them ideas for improvements in their own area.

There are many ways to publicize success. For example, you could use the following:

- ☞ "Brag-boards" in high traffic areas
- ☞ Quarterly meetings
- ☞ Newsletters
- ☞ Memos or electronic mail

Step 15

Step 15: Disband the team.

You might *think* this an obvious step that no one could forget. **Wrong!** Often sponsors keep a team together just in case there are loose ends to tie up later; then they forget to disband it formally. Team members need closure. Personally write to each of them, thanking them for their time and effort and relieving them of their duties to the project. It does not have to be a formal letter; a handwritten note will do—just enough to say thank you as well as to give closure to the project.

If you have completed all your practice exercises and have a draft charter in your hands, you are ready to take on your team sponsor role.

CHAPTER 2

SPONSORING A STANDING TEAM

If you think you're ready to take on a standing team, it's time to get going and meet the challenge. You have a lot of work to do to get your standing team started. But again, before you begin setting up the team, you must ask yourself three key questions.

	Yes	No	I Don't Know
1. Am I sure this is a long-term, recurring issue that can best be addressed by a team?	❑	❑	❑
2. Am I sure this **cannot** be broken down into short-term issues that ad hoc teams could address?	❑	❑	❑
3. If this will take a lot of time or resources, am I sure that it fits into the facility's priorities? That is, can I justify it?	❑	❑	❑

If your answer to any of these questions is "no," do not set up a standing team! If your answer is "I don't know," then get to work—you have to go looking for some answers before you can proceed any further. But let's look very carefully at each of these questions before you answer with a definite "yes."

Question 1

If this is a recurring, long-term issue that can best be addressed by one person, assign one person to it. But if the issue requires the input of different backgrounds or disciplines, and if the successful implementation of plans requires the "buy-in" of members, then answer "yes" to question one.

Question 2

Standing teams generally do not have a specific, concrete goal. As a result, they do not get the same sense of accomplishment or challenge that comes from an ad hoc team. For members to gain a sense of achievement, they must be able to spin off some specific shorter term goals that move them toward their overall mission; otherwise, you may end up with a frustrated team.

If it is possible to take the issue and break it down into smaller, short-term, achievable goals, you may be better off sponsoring several ad hoc teams. But if you are sure that this is an overall mission that the organization must strive toward whether or not it actually reaches the goal, answer "yes" to question two.

Question 3

You must be absolutely certain that if the team comes up with recommendations, procedures, and the like you will be able to "sell" them. You may be setting the team up for failure if the issue does not have high priority within the overall facility priorities. Remember, the purpose of a standing team is to continually dedicate resources to a particular issue. Be sure that you can justify it! Only then can you answer "yes" to question three.

So **do not** go on unless you are completely sure about your answers to these questions. Only if you can answer "yes" without a doubt in your mind should you begin setting the foundation in place for your standing team.

SPONSOR'S CHECKLIST FOR STANDING TEAMS

TASK TO BE COMPLETED	✓ Check When Complete
1. Draft the team's overall mission, the boundaries, and the resources available.	❑
2. Meet with the teams coordinator and have a facilitator assigned.	❑
3. Review the draft with the facilitator and make any needed revisions.	❑
4. Appoint a team leader.	❑
5. Determine team membership and composition rules with input from the team leader.	❑
6. Ensure there is a meeting with each team member to gain their support for the team.	❑
7. Meet with team member's supervisor to ensure support for the team.	❑
8. Complete the charter form.	❑
9. Give the team a chance to suggest and clarify charter revisions, to decide rotation rules, and to set operating guidelines.	❑
10. Publish final version of the charter, including the mission statement, operating guidelines, and rotational rules.	❑
11. Actively monitor the team's progress.	❑
12. Ensure that the team is developing goals that help accomplish the mission; ensure that its metrics support its goals.	❑
13. Get resources as needed for the team to implement decisions, policies, and procedures.	❑

Step 1: Draft the team's overall mission, boundaries, and available resources.

The charter for a standing team includes the following elements:

1. **The mission of the team**
2. **The boundaries**
3. **The budget and other available resources**
4. **Composition rules**
5. **Rotational rules**

The last two elements are developed with input from the team. However, your first step as sponsor is to draft the first three. Here's an example of a sponsor's draft.

THE SAFETY STANDING TEAM

Mission — The purpose of the Safety Standing Team is to create an environment in which employees are free from injuries.

Boundaries
- This team **may not** change safety policies without approval from the Plant Steering Team.
- This team **may** implement safety awareness programs and incentives within their budget.
- This team **may** conduct safety audits in any department without notice.
- This team **may** require a department or supervisor to change a safety practice.

Budget or Other Resources
- $10,000 for safety awards program
- Word processing support from human resources department
- Three team members may attend annual safety conference

☞ *Note:*

The biggest difference between an ad hoc team and a standing team's charter is that for an ad hoc team, the goals and objectives are very clearly stated. It is the sponsor's job to ensure there is little need for interpretation. In contrast, the standing team's charge is very broad. It becomes the team's job to develop the specific goals and objectives that support the broad mission. The sponsor must review and monitor those goals and objectives, ensuring that they do support the mission as the sponsor intended and that the metrics support the goal.

You've seen how we do it—now it's your turn to write a standing team's mission statement, boundaries, and budget and other resources. This time, the "expert" answers will immediately follow the exercise, along with some helpful comments.

Exercise — Sponsor's Draft

Draft the mission, boundaries, and resources for the following team:

You are the assistant plant manager. You are concerned that there is little communication from shift to shift and no face-to-face contact at shift change. You want the shift managers to meet on a regular basis to improve communication, solve shared problems, and increase the cooperation from shift to shift.

 1. *What is the overall mission of this team? What are the recurring, critical issues that you want this team to deal with?*

(Continued)

Exercise — Sponsor's Draft *(Continued)*

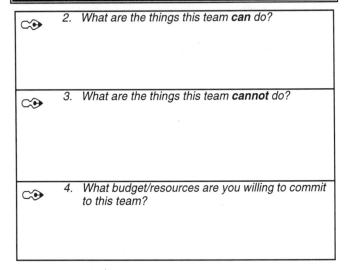

2. What are the things this team **can** do?

3. What are the things this team **cannot** do?

4. What budget/resources are you willing to commit to this team?

Now compare your answers to the "expert" examples below and on the following page.

1. What is the overall mission of this team? What are the recurring, critical issues that you want this team to deal with?

The mission of the Shift Coordination Team is to improve the communication, coordination, and cooperation among the three production shifts.

This is a broad statement of the team's purpose. Notice that it is a "pie in the sky" kind of goal. Communication, coordination, and cooperation are issues that multi-shift operations will always struggle with. The team's goal is to constantly strive toward further improvement.

Exercise — Sponsor's Draft *(Continued)*

2. What are the things this team *can* do?

The team may change their working hours if needed.
The team may meet on any shift they choose.
The team must meet at least once a week.
The team may include production employees in their
meetings.
The team may make recommendations about electronic
means of communication.

The sponsor, in deciding on the boundaries, includes one of her "musts" on this list. She also includes precisely what the team can recommend so that the team's authority will not overlap with that of another team.

3. What are the things this team *cannot* do?

The team cannot change the working hours of associates.
The team cannot purchase any electronic or computerized
means of communication without approval of the
information management team.

The list of "cannots" is shorter—the sponsor again specifies that the team's authority cannot overlap with that of another team.

4. What budget/resources are you willing to commit to this team?

Sponsor A: *$0*

(If recommendations requiring money are accepted, the team
will negotiate a budget with the team sponsor)

(Continued)

Exercise — Sponsor's Draft (Continued)

Sponsor B:

The team may include the plant manager or department heads at any of their meetings.

The team may include production associates in meetings on overtime if needed.

The team may use the production manager's secretary for clerical support if needed.

Sponsor A does not see a need for a budget, although she does let team members know that they can negotiate a budget if needed.

Sponsor B sees people as a resource. She wants to ensure that team members know whom they can include in their meetings and under what conditions.

How did your ideas compare? Remember, your ideas did not have to be exactly like the experts' to be right. Review the exercise with your facilitator and get his or her reaction to your ideas.

Now that you're as good as the "experts," it's time to take a stab at drafting your team's mission, boundaries, and resources.

Exercise — Your Turn

👉 *What is the overall mission of the team? What recurring, critical issues do I want the team to deal with?*

_____

_____

_____

(Continued)

Exercise — Your Turn *(Concluded)*

↪ *What are the things this team **can** do?*

_____

_____

_____

↪ *What are the things this team **cannot** do?*

_____

_____

_____

↪ *What budget am I willing to commit to the team?*

_____

_____

_____

↪ *What resources am I willing to commit to this team?*

_____

_____

_____

You now have a draft of the team charter's first three elements:

  1. **The mission of the team**

  2. **The boundaries**

  3. **The budget and other available resources**

Step 2
Step 2: Meet with the teams coordinator and have a facilitator assigned.

Now that you have your first draft in hand, it's time to go looking for some help. Meet with the teams coordinator first to ensure that the team and mission you have in mind does not overlap with the mission of an existing team. Once you are certain that there is no overlap, have a facilitator assigned to your team. If there is a facilitator with whom you work well, let the coordinator know that.

Step 3
Step 3: Review the draft with the facilitator; make any needed revisions.

Show the facilitator the draft that you developed in Step 1. Your facilitator has probably had many opportunities to hone his or her skills in writing clear statements. Take advantage of that expertise. Have the facilitator help you review, revise, and edit your first draft. He or she may have some innovative ideas about boundaries and resources that you haven't thought of.

Step 4
Step 4: Appoint the team leader.

There are several factors to consider in appointing the team leader:

➤ It should be someone who is knowledgeable about or responsible for the function for which the team is chartered.
➤ It should be someone who is respected by peers and can lead a team without taking over.
➤ It should be someone who is knowledgeable about the organization and can provide any needed help.
➤ It should be someone who has the time it will take to get this team off the ground and going in the right direction.

The last factor is probably the most critical. If the team leader does not have enough time to devote to the team's activities, you will end up with a real problem. Never appoint someone the leader without first asking the person about his or her other commitments, including the number of teams currently served on. You should also talk to the person's supervisor, ensuring that no upcoming projects or assignments will interfere with team priorities.

 Step 5: Determine team membership and composition rules with input from the team leader.

Together you and the team leader must determine who should be on the team. The following questions may help.

- What areas or functions will this issue have an impact on?
- What areas would have to carry out decisions, policies, or procedures developed by this team?
- What other areas or functions might have special knowledge or expertise on this issue?

Use the answers to these questions to identify the necessary membership. Remember! We don't want teams to be too big— the rule of thumb is no less than three, no more than 10.

Also, make sure you choose team members who will have the time to spend on team activities, who will be motivated to work on the issue, who have an interest in the issue, and who are not serving on too many other teams. You or the team leader will get a chance to address these concerns in Step 6.

 Step 6: Ensure that there is a meeting with each team member to gain their support for the team.

Even if you bring together the smartest, best-suited group of people in the world for your team, they won't be successful if they don't have the time to spend on the project. By meeting with each team member, or by having the team leader do it, you can gauge the member's level of commitment to, and interest in, the project. You also can find out whether he or she is serving on any other teams.

Step 7 Step 7: Meet with each team member's supervisor to ensure support for the team.

When asking people to serve on a standing team, you must be certain that their supervisors are willing to free up enough time for them to spend on the project. Try to give a member's supervisor some idea of the project's time frame so that he or she can realistically assess whether this person has the time needed to follow through on the team commitment.

Step 8 Step 8: Complete the charter form.

Finally! It's time to take all the decisions you've made so far and capture them on the charter form. Turn to Appendix A to see an example of a completed standing team charter; then complete the blank charter form on the following page.

Step 9 Step 9: Give the team a chance to suggest and clarify charter revisions, rotational rules, and to set operating guidelines.

At this point, a meeting is essential. Keep in mind that the team has yet to set specific goals, objectives, or measures. Its members need a chance to understand their overall mission and to get clear on the amount of time needed to serve on the team. You can give them this chance in a number of ways. For example:

front end can buy you commitment, thorough understanding, and a smoother ride for the team's duration. And don't forget: a standing team is a permanent team. The way it is started can set the tone for the life of the team.

The final version of the charter needs to go into a team logbook. Using this logbook, the team can organize and document its activities, including agendas, action minutes, and parking lot forms (all filed sequentially). The logbook also helps you identify the roadblocks or barriers that the team has run up against. Identifying those roadblocks is a first step toward removing them.

Congratulations!

You've done your job in getting the team started on the right track. You have sponsored a standing team that has a firm footing and a strong foundation.

But your job is not over. You must actively monitor the team and stay involved in providing it with appropriate resources. You also must review and approve the goals and metrics that the team will develop. The last three tasks in your sponsor's checklist will give you the guidance you need to support your team in these ways. Let's review those tasks now.

TASK TO BE COMPLETED	✓ Check When Complete
11. Actively monitor the team's progress.	☐
12. Ensure that the team is developing goals that help accomplish the mission; ensure that its metrics support its goals.	☐
13. Get the resources the team needs to implement decisions, policies, and procedures.	☐

A standing team is a long-term proposal—and you have to play a long-term role. Steps 11 through 13 are never-ending tasks. The checklist format will remind you to keep at them, for they are not things you can actually check off as completed. You will have to carry out these activities repeatedly, until you are no longer the sponsor of the team.

Step 11 Step 11: Actively monitor the team's progress.

It is up to team members to determine what activities will help them meet their mission. It is up to you to make sure that you understand how these activities help them in working toward that mission. The mission of a standing team is a vision, a quest, a desired state that the team is striving for but will never actually reach. Members must decide what activities will help them reach this "never-never land," and sometimes they have difficulty deciding where to focus their resources and energy. Therefore it is important, particularly at the beginning of the team's development, that you actively monitor the team's activities. To do this, you can use several methods:

1. Periodically attend meetings.

2. Review the team logbook frequently.

3. Meet regularly with the facilitator or team leader.

4. Act as sponsor for resulting ad hoc teams.

Step 12 Step 12: Ensure that the team is developing goals that help accomplish the mission; ensure that its metrics support its goals.

Standing teams must develop short-term goals and objectives in order to meet their overall mission or purpose. There are three different approaches that a team can take to accomplish these short-term goals:

- All members may act as an ad hoc team working toward the goal.

- The team may spin off subteams to act as ad hoc teams working on the goal.

- The team may sponsor an ad hoc team made up of members from other areas of the organization.

If your team selects either the first or the second approach, you automatically become the sponsor of the resulting ad hoc team. It is your responsibility to ensure that metrics are in place to support the goal and that the team has the necessary resources. In the event that the team sponsors an ad hoc team, they are responsible for negotiating the necessary resources with you. Make sure that they understand this on the front end.

When ad hoc teams are used, the goals must be reviewed from four angles:

1. Does the goal actually move the team toward the overall, chartered mission?

2. Where do the priorities for this goal fit into those of other goals that the team might be working on?

3. Is the goal clear and specific?

4. Does the metric support the goal?

Questions one and two are judgment calls. Are you comfortable with the activity that team members have chosen to focus their efforts on? Do you understand their reasons for choosing this goal? If you prioritized all the activities they could be working on, would this be high on the list?

Questions three and four are more objective. In our discussion of ad hoc teams, we covered the criteria for good, clear, specific goal statements and metrics that support the goal. A good goal statement is clear and specific and includes some measure of what you want the team to accomplish (expected outcomes). You can find examples of goal statements early on in Chapter 1.

You must also make sure that the team has appropriate metrics. Remember the three rules of metrics?

> **Rule 1. The metrics must follow the goal statement.**
> **Rule 2. Not every team will need to use the metrics planning table.**
> **Rule 3. The metrics are *not* the data the team needs to solve its problem.**

If you feel the need for a quick review, turn to the section "Step 11" in Chapter 1. If you are not satisfied with the team's goals and metrics, ask the facilitator to conduct a team training session in goal writing and metric development. You might even sit in on the training to show support for the team's activities and to sharpen your own skills.

Okay—enough lecturing. It's time for you to move on to the next exercise and try your hand at reviewing some short-term goals developed by a standing team.

Exercise — Reviewing Short-Term Goals

Review the QI Team's short-term goals from the four angles you have learned about, and answer the questions that follow.

The Quality Improvement Team

The overall purpose of the Quality Improvement Team is to monitor, evaluate, and improve the quality procedures throughout the plant.

Short-Term Goal 1:
To ensure that every employee understands the eight steps of the quality improvement process

The team has developed this metric:

Every employee will have completed a four-hour training session on the quality improvement process by March 15.

☞	1. Does the goal/objective support the overall purpose of the team? Why or why not?
☞	2. Does the metric measure accomplishment of the goal? Why or why not?

Short-Term Goal 2:
To ensure that operators are following standard operating procedures (SOP).

The team has developed this metric:

Audit 50% of the production operators at their job sites, across all three shifts, checking for knowledge of SOPs and use of SOPs.

	1. Does the goal/objective support the overall purpose of the team? Why or why not?
	2. Does the metric measure accomplishment of the goal? Why or why not?

Now compare your work to the sample answers given in Appendix B.

Step 13

Step 13: Get resources as needed for the team to implement decisions, policies, and procedures.

As the sponsor, it is your responsibility to get resources for the team. Sometimes the resources may be dollars; other times they may be people or hours of your time; and occasionally they may be your efforts to go to bat for the team. Remember those questions you asked yourself before starting the team? You believed that the issue was important enough to warrant the efforts of team members over a long period of time. Now you must follow through and prove your decision to be the right one.

If team members come up with recommendations that you have to fight for, make sure that they understand what data, supporting documentation, or cost figures you need from them to make a convincing argument. It is their job to arm you with what you need to go into battle; it is your job to pull off the victory.

You might need these types of ammo:

➤ Cost-benefit analysis

➤ Dollar figures on what the problem is costing

➤ Amount of scrap/waste generated by the problem

➤ Amount of lost or nonproductive time caused by the problem

➤ Alternative, less costly methods of implementing the idea (a backup plan)

➤ Ways to implement the idea over a period of time

You can work to implement the team's decisions in the following ways:

☞ Go to your boss armed with the information provided by the team.

☞ Get on the agenda for the annual budget meeting armed with information provided by the team.

☞ Schedule a meeting with department managers who will be affected by the idea and see if they are willing to share the financial burden between departments.

Congratulations! You have a draft of a standing team charter in your hands now. You are ready to carry out Steps 2 through 10 of the checklist in order to build a solid foundation for your team. However, your work has only just begun when you complete Step 10.

Steps 11, 12, and 13 will continue to be a part of your job for as long as you remain the sponsor of the standing team. If there was a time when you worried that teams would strip you of a role in the organization, be reassured. The team sponsor role is just one of the many roles you will continue to play for a very long time.

CHAPTER 3

SPONSORING A NATURAL TEAM

Now you're ready to tackle a natural team, the toughest one so far.

Again, you must ask yourself three key questions before you start up the team.

QUESTION	Yes	No	I Don't Know
1. Is there potential for improving the business or the way work is performed by developing teams in this area?	☐	☐	☐
2. Is this a stable work area with little to medium turnover in employees?	☐	☐	☐
3. Is this an area in which natural groups can be easily configured into units of fewer than 10 people?	☐	☐	☐

A "yes" answer to question one is critical to the success of your team. If employees cannot see any reason or benefit from change, they resist it. Often there is resistance even when the benefit is clear! You'll have a tough time getting employees' "buy in" if no real improvement can be gained through the use of teamwork.

You must be able to answer "yes" to question two as well. An area with high turnover is very difficult to transform into a high-performance work team. When team composition changes frequently over short periods of time, the team is essentially starting over again each time membership changes.

Question three is simply about logistics. When you have many people performing the same tasks, it is very difficult to divide the workforce into logical small groupings. Even if you are able to make some kind of logical grouping, you may find yourself with four or five teams all performing the same job but in different ways. These teams often find themselves at odds with one another. When teams have common problems, they usually have different ideas about how to solve the problem. Each team gets "locked on" to their way of solving it, and team-to-team conflict occurs. In these cases, it may be more beneficial to use a standing team instead of a natural team.

WHAT IS A NATURAL TEAM?

Before we can talk about how to sponsor natural teams, we must know the defining features of such teams.

> A natural team is a group whose members perform interrelated or interdependent tasks; by members working together cooperatively, the performance of those tasks is improved or enhanced. The tasks may be organized around a product, process, or customer.

Essentially, a natural team is a natural work group. However, this does not mean that every natural work group will automatically be a successful natural team.

Before you convert a natural work group into a team, you must consider the way the group is currently operating. Often work is broken up into very individualized tasks. An employee's success or failure depends on the performance of a single task, and shares no interdependency with the performance of other work-group members; in fact, the employee may know little or nothing about other members' responsibilities. In such a case, you will have a tough time taking the work group and making it a team without changing something about its tasks or its measures. Sometimes the change is simply a matter of increasing employee knowledge and awareness of what others are doing; at other times, the actual work must be reconfigured.

If the interdependency or interrelatedness is not obvious, you will need to examine your options for reorganizing the work area. Some managers form design teams, made up of the area employees, to evaluate the jobs. Some companies go through the entire plant, re-engineering jobs and processes. Other companies look at small areas or pockets and design pilot teams. Whatever method your plant or company uses, you're probably going to have to live with it. Contact your teams coordinator to find out what type of help is available in setting up your natural team.

One rule of thumb to remember: wherever possible, involve the people who do the jobs. They are likely to have all kinds of ideas! You may be able to configure your teams with a few small changes, or you may have to go through major restructuring. Whatever you do, keep these guidelines in mind:

- ➤ Keep teams small in size—no fewer than three, no more than 10 team members.
- ➤ If possible, construct teams so that internal suppliers and internal customers are on the same team.
- ➤ If possible, select as members those people who provide critical support to the team.
- ➤ Try to keep natural team members working in relative geographic proximity to each other.

The above are **general** guidelines. In configuring your team, you may have to make some trade-offs and that's okay. There are no set rules about the makeup of your team.

THE FOUR LEVELS OF TEAM DEVELOPMENT

There are four levels of development that every natural team must master. Your role changes significantly as the team works its way through each level. Your challenge is to determine when the team is ready to move on to the next level, and to change your role accordingly. Let's look at the four levels.

LEVEL	PHASE
One	**Foundation**. In this phase of development, the team focuses on mastering team-building skills, meeting skills, and basic team processes. Members learn to take ownership of their tasks and work to improve the processes they control. The focus of team activities is to learn to accomplish day-to-day activities interdependently and cooperatively.
Two	**Business Focus**. In this phase, the team begins to align its mission and efforts with the facility's priorities and to develop achievable goals that will advance the team toward those priorities. Members learn to sponsor subteams or ad hoc teams to help them in achieving the team's specific goals. The focus of team activities is on critical business initiatives and improving their processes in order to meet those initiatives.
Three	**Increased Responsibility**. At this level, the natural team gradually begins to make more of the decisions that affect its work. The areas of responsibility granted to the team are carefully chosen and planned. The team will often have less need for a facilitator at this level. The supervisor may begin the transition from the role of facilitator—usually becoming more of a technical advisor and coach.
Four	**Shared Leadership**. During level four, the team becomes "self-managed." The team requires little or no traditional supervision. Most of the roles of the traditional supervisor will be assumed by the members themselves. For level-four teams, the supervisor no longer functions in the traditional role, but instead has become a facilitator or has taken on some other role in the organization.

Your Role as the Sponsor

As you work your way through this chapter, you will see that there are two distinct aspects of your role as the sponsor:

1. Structuring the team so that they get started in the right direction

2. "Growing" or developing the team through the four levels

Section A will deal with how to structure or set up the team. Section B will concentrate on your role in developing the team once it is underway.

SECTION A: GETTING TEAMS STARTED

Level-one teams must concentrate on learning how to get their daily activities completed cooperatively. They focus most of their efforts on improving communication, interpersonal relationships, and cooperative task sharing. Your job is to set the stage for team members to learn these basic teamwork skills and to make small improvements in their processes. Let's look at where you focus your time and efforts when at level one.

LEVEL ONE — SPONSOR'S ROLE

- Plays a strong, visible role
- Talks to the facilitator frequently, getting reports on the processes that the team is using, the issues that members are spending their efforts on, and the level of participation that is occurring
- Regularly reviews the minutes of team meetings
- Meets with the team leader or team spokesperson
- Ensures that the team is following up on decisions by reviewing action minutes
- Sets the goals
- Ensures that the team is staying within its focus of control and working on issues that have immediate impact and are easy to implement

As you can see, the sponsor plays a highly active role in developing and maintaining level-one teams; he or she provides the team with a strong structure. Natural teams are quite different from the other two teams we have discussed. With either a standing team or an ad hoc team, the sponsor ensures that members are motivated, committed people. With  a natural team, however, the sponsor must deal with those already in the jobs. Membership is not voluntary; everyone who works in the area must be on the team. Thus the sponsor's real issue is "How do I 'grow' this group of people?" Your job as sponsor is to become a change agent, and to do that, you must set a strong direction for the team from the start and then learn to back off as the team gets rolling.

Below are the steps for getting your team started on the right track. However, **once you get the team started, there are no easy checklists to guide you**; it becomes a matter of truly learning how to manage people.

SPONSOR'S CHECKLIST FOR NATURAL TEAMS

Tasks to Be Completed	✓ Check when Complete
1. Go to the teams coordinator and have a facilitator assigned.	❑
2. Write the charter—including overall responsibilities, job description, decision-making authority, and empowerment limits.	❑
3. Review performance measures and adapt if needed.	❑

(Continued)

Tasks to Be Completed *(Continued)*	✓ Check when Complete
4. Appoint the team leader.	❑
5. Meet with the team to review the charter.	❑
6. Arrange for team training.	❑
7. Have the team write its mission statement and develop operating guidelines.	❑
8. Monitor and evaluate team results.	❑

Step 1: Go to the teams coordinator and have a facilitator assigned.

Before you get started, go to the teams coordinator and find out what resources are available to help you through this process. The reality is, whatever you do must fit your company's overall priorities and resources—and there will certainly be some limitations on how you can structure the team and what resources are available. So go to the teams coordinator at the start, find out what your facility's do's and don'ts are, and have a facilitator assigned to work with you through the process.

Step 2: Write the charter—including overall responsibilities, job descriptions, decision-making authority, and empowerment limits.

As the sponsor, your job is to ensure that the team members know exactly what is expected of them. As you learned earlier, the charter is the document that you use to communicate your expectations. An example of a completed natural team charter is provided in Appendix A. Note that the charter must include the following:

1. Overall purpose of the team:

The charter needs to include the broad business purpose of the work group.

> Example: To produce widgets that meet or exceed the quality standards of ABC company

2. The team's responsibilities:

The charter must also include the specific tasks, duties, and responsibilities that you expect the team to take ownership of.

> Example: Preventive maintenance, keeping internal customers supplied, housekeeping, break coverage, quality inspections.

3. Decisions to be made, along with the limits on those decisions:

At this point, you do not want to overwhelm the team by giving members too much responsibility. But you do want to begin building ownership for the work process by granting minimal decision-making responsibility.

Example:

(a) Team members will write work orders when machinery needs maintenance.

> *Limits:* If the necessary repair will affect production, supervisor must be notified immediately after work order is turned in.

(b) Team members will determine when to break and how to cover work area during breaks.

> *Limits:* Breaks may be taken any time between 11:00 a.m. and 2:00 p.m. At least two team members must be in work area at all times.

The Planning Session table on the next page will help you determine which decisions the team members must be able to make in order to carry out their jobs effectively and efficiently.

PLANNING SESSION

TASK OR RESPONSIBILITY	DECISION REQUIRED	EMPOWERMENT LIMITS	PERSON TEAM CAN TURN TO FOR EXPERTISE	TRAINING NEEDED
Cover breaks during the shift	Determine how team members will cover breaks	• Machines must run during breaks • No breaks during first and last hour of the shift • Must always have at least three operators in the area	John McMillan (supervisor)	None
Cover each other's jobs during vacation/absenteeism	Determine rotation schedule for overtime	• No one can work more than 16 hours per day	John McMillan	Finish all cross training of associates
Conduct preventative maintenance tasks that must be carried out between the regularly scheduled overhauls	Determine schedule and assignments for carrying out preventative maintenance tasks	• Each task must be completed as frequently as stated in manual • Must complete the check-off list on a weekly basis	Gary Long (maintenance superintendent)	Four hours of training in preventative maintenance
Serve on safety committee and ad hoc teams	Determine which team member will serve on which teams	• No overtime without approval • No workflow disruptions	Gene Lowe (department manager)	None

Notice that most of the decisions are related to how the team members get their activities accomplished. This is the appropriate focus for level-one teams. Remember, such teams are trying to master working together on day-in, day-out activities. At this stage you are not trying to "release power"; instead, your goal is to turn over the decisions that members need to be making to get their jobs accomplished. These are decisions that supervisors or specialists have been making and that probably should have been turned over to the employees as they gained experience in their jobs. By turning these things over to the team, you are beginning to build ownership.

 Step 3: Review measures and adapt if needed.

If you have changed the way that the work is carried out, then the old performance measures are probably not appropriate. Even if you haven't changed anything about the work, you want to take a good look at the team's performance measures. Teams without measures are like travelers without a map: if they reach their final destination, it will be by pure luck. By ensuring that they know what their key performance measures are, you are not leaving things to chance. You must also ensure they understand that they are responsible for tracking those measures and for taking action when they are not meeting those measures.

There are four basic categories of performance measures:

- **Quality**
- **Quantity**
- **Timeliness**
- **Cost**

Of course, there are guidelines you should keep in mind as you decide on the team's performance measures. Take a look at the following tests of good measures.

1. The measures must be stated in easily understood terms that team members relate to.

The measures must be something that team members relate to their daily activities—something that they rally around. Using a measure that is stated in accounting terms, such as percentage of variance to standard cost budgeting, will mean little to team members. But if the measure is stated in terms of pounds of waste/scrap, team members will know exactly what it means and will be able to relate their activities to that measure.

2. The measure must be of value-added activities.

Obviously, you only want to measure things that matter. Measures are what the team members will focus their attention on. However, organizations sometimes measure for the sake of measuring. Make sure that if performance on this factor varies, it really makes a difference in the final outcome.

3. The measures must support the department/ organization's mission.

The purpose of measures is to help the team move closer to the departmental goal or mission. A logical question, then, of all measures is "Does this move us closer to our vision?" As the sponsor, you must have a clear understanding of the overall goals and mission of the department. If team members are focusing their efforts on activities that do not have an impact on the critical result areas of the department, then you are on the wrong track with your team's performance factors.

4. The measures must be factors within the team's control.

If the measures are beyond the team's control, you are going to have a very frustrated team. If the measurements are strongly affected by suppliers or outside factors or support, you have the wrong measures.

5. The measures must be customer-focused.

Your team's customer may be internal or external. Either way, if the team's performance measures are not connected to how well they supply products, services, or information to their customer, the needs of the final, external customer will be affected. Ask yourself, Who gets this team's output, and what are their critical requirements? Your measures must tie back to these critical requirements.

6. The data must be accessible to the team.

If the information is not easily accessed by the team, members are less likely to make it the focus of their attention. The data should be collected and charted by the team.

It's time for you to try reviewing some team performance measures by completing the following exercise.

Exercise — Performance Measures

Situation A

A banking operation's measures are based on volume of items processed within a day's time. Each team has a certain amount of volume that they have to meet for the week. Some work is easier and faster to process than other work, and often the teams process the easiest work first. However, the customer is paying for and expecting timely deposit of items. Management is very frustrated by the fact that the oldest work is not being processed first.

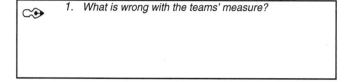

1. What is wrong with the teams' measure?

2. What measures would you suggest for the teams? Why?

Situation B

The mission statement for the materials management department in a widget factory is as follows:

Our goal is to provide internal customers with necessary supplies and parts on time, every time. One hundred percent of parts delivered will meet customer requirements.

The following measures are in place for the team responsible for supplying the production floor with widget parts:

- Percentage of parts delivered to user departments on time

- Number of production delays due to unavailability of necessary parts

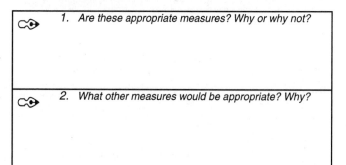

1. Are these appropriate measures? Why or why not?

2. What other measures would be appropriate? Why?

Now compare your work to the sample answers given in Appendix B.

In addition to having the right measures for your team, you need good baseline data. Baseline data is important for two reasons:

1. It allows you to document the improvements that you accomplish through the team. (Remember—success leads to more success.)

2. With baseline data, you can set challenging but achievable goals; it helps you assess current conditions, so that you know how much improvement is needed.

You may be able to put together baseline data from historical data for the area. If not, one of the first tasks of the team may be to collect baseline data.

Step 4: Appoint a team leader.

In level-one teams, the team leader's role is primarily that of a meeting leader, although he or she may help coordinate assignments in the work setting as well. The supervisor typically remains in the traditional supervisory role, helping to resolve conflict, dealing with human resource issues, and handling discipline. The team leader's responsibilities are to ensure participation and involvement in team projects and team meetings, to make sure that the team is using good processes, and to help keep the team focused on key performance measures. When trying to determine whom to choose as the team leader, ask yourself these questions:

➤ Do team members look up to and respect this person?

➤ Does this person do his or her share of the work willingly?

➤ Is this person willing to seek help when needed?

➤ Is this person well organized and a good communicator?

➤ Is this person strong enough to refocus the team if members stray into inappropriate areas?

➤ Can this person coordinate and lead without becoming a "mini-supervisor"?

The leadership role will probably rotate once the team members are comfortable with the meeting processes and their new roles. However, it is essential that the first team leader be carefully selected, because he or she often sets the tone and the model for others. It is also important that the team leader assume the role long enough to learn and become comfortable with it. The length of time will depend on the group's maturity and experience level. For a group that has had little experience in leadership roles, the initial rotation should last between six and nine months. If the group has experience in leadership, you may want to rotate more frequently; but you would probably not want to rotate any more frequently than monthly under any circumstances.

Step 5: Meet with the team to review the charter.

Once the charter has been written, you must sit down with the team to go over duties, responsibilities, and measures, making it clear that all members of the team are equally responsible for efficient and effective performance of those duties. It is also important to communicate any expectations you have for the team. For example, if you expect the team to meet at a regularly scheduled time and place, let members know that up front. If you expect the team to have short huddle-type meetings on a daily basis, state that in clear terms. If there are certain things that you insist on being informed of immediately (machinery breakdowns, coverage issues, and so on), communicate that expectation.

It is critical that you review the team's decision-making responsibilities carefully. It is your job to ensure that there are no misunderstandings about what the team can and cannot do in the area of decision making. One of the quickest ways to kill a team's motivation is to let members think they have more empowerment than they do, and then pull back after the fact.

Step 6: Arrange for team training.

Everyone on the team must have training in meeting processes before the team begins operating. For those whose skills may be rusty, make sure that brush-up training takes place. It is very effective to combine the training with the meeting to review the team's charter. The trainer reviews the meeting processes and then you conduct the meeting. It gives you the opportunity to "walk the talk" by modeling the meeting behaviors that you expect from the team.

 Step 7: Have the team write its mission statement and develop operating guidelines.

Writing the Mission Statement

The team now needs to meet on its own. At this meeting, members should write a mission statement for their group, develop their ground rules, and come up with their operating guidelines. Members must have a copy of the department mission statement before they begin working on the team's mission statement. It is critical that they align their mission statement to the department's. Here are four questions that may help team members develop their mission statement:

QUESTION	↔	SAMPLE
1. What do we do? What are our processes	↔	Make widgets
2. Who are our customers?	↔	Consumer, packaging department
3. What level of quality do we strive for?	↔	The most efficient and long-lasting
4. How do we act towards each other?	↔	Communicate openly/honestly; treat each other with respect

For an example of a team's mission statement, see Appendix C.

To help the team write its mission statement, give each member a worksheet like the one below, distributing the copies before the first team meeting. Each member writes down his or her thoughts and brings the sheet to the meeting. Using a round-robin format, all ideas are captured on the flipchart. Members discuss the ideas after they are recorded and make appropriate combinations. The next step is to rank order the statements. Once the statements are ranked, the highest-rated statements are edited into an easily understood, brief statement that serves as a rallying call for the team.

WORKSHEET — WRITING YOUR MISSION STATEMENT

Mission statements are important because they state the direction your team is supposed to head in. They serve as a lantern, guiding your tasks and activities as a team.

What is the purpose of your team?

As a team, your mission is most likely to produce a product, perform an operation on an existing product, or to offer a service to some internal or external customer.

Write down three to five reasons why your team exists. What is your team supposed to accomplish or be responsible for? Who is your customer?

_____

Write down some words that describe the way you would want your level of quality to be viewed by your customer.

_____

Write down some words that describe how you want your team members to behave towards each other.

_____

Developing Ground Rules

The team must develop its own ground rules without your input. However, you can suggest the following method. Members start by brainstorming a list of the ways they **do not** want to act in meetings. From that list, they come up with a corresponding set of ground rules. The ground rules should be posted in the team's meeting room and should be included in the logbook. Ground rules are included in Appendix C.

Developing Operating Guidelines

The team must also develop a set of operating guidelines. Here are some items that might be included in the guidelines:

- Where, how often, and when the team plans to meet
- How they rotate responsibilities—both in meetings and on the work floor
- Who the team contacts for assistance (i.e., maintenance contact, purchasing contact)
- How the team communicates with other shifts
- How the team communicates with other teams
- Team members' names and how to contact each member

Basically, the team's operating guidelines lay out how members plan to get their work completed. For an example of operating guidelines, see Appendix C.

Step 8: Monitor and evaluate team results.

As you learned in Chapters 1 and 2, your work has just begun when you start your team. The principle applies here too: you must keep a natural team on the right track once you get it started. This is particularly important for level-one teams. Try using the following methods to monitor and evaluate your team.

ughest part of your job is identifying when the team is
to move on. Many teams progress quickly in some areas
ruggle in others. There are no clear-cut lines between the
—the team may be operating at level three in one area,
early remain at level one in another. You and the
ator must work together to help the team focus on the
that need improvement and to encourage members in
nastery of the areas in which they excel.

section will be organized by what you can expect to see in
am at each level and what your role is in helping
bers master each level and move on to the next.

start by getting a "macro" view. Review the chart on the
ving page showing your role at each level. Notice how it
ges over time. You can see that you start out very actively
essen your presence over time. By the time the team
s it to level four, your role is minimal—you provide
iical advice if needed and you only step in when asked.

LEVEL ONE

u have given your team a lot of direction, structure, and
ance, they should be able to master level one without a lot
fficulties.

e are no set rules about how long a team stays at level one.
t depends on the members' degree of sophistication. The
wing factors affect the length of time it takes the team to
ress to level two:

➤ Have the team members participated in meetings in
the past?

➤ Do they have good interactive skills?

➤ Do they have good problem-solving and
communication skills?

➤ Was there much employee involvement prior to the
team?

➤ What was the trust level between management and
employees prior to the teams?

1. Have the team decide how they will track and report their key performance measures to you.

This should be the team's first task. Let members know if you have any minimum time frames that you expect in terms of getting reports. Tracking the team's performance through hard data is your best tool for evaluating their progress and monitoring their results.

2. Review the team logbook.

All natural teams should have a logbook. If possible, every member should have a copy of his or her own. If this is not an option, then the team leader should keep up with the team's copy. This logbook should include the following:

- Charter
- Operating guidelines
- Copies of all agendas
- Copies of parking lot forms

- Mission statement
- Ground rules
- Copies of all action minutes
- Master copies of all forms

The logbook will help keep the team organized, help members focus on their business purpose, and give you one place to go to monitor the team's development. The agendas will tell you whether the team is spending its time on the right things; action minutes will let you see whether members are equally involved (the "assigned to" column should have a variety of names in it if all members are getting involved); parking lots will show you whether the team is following up or letting things fall through the cracks. Action minutes are also a good place to see what the team has been able to accomplish. The status column will show you accomplishments in one glance.

As mentioned in Chapter 1, examples of the three types of forms appear in Appendix C.

3. Meet with the team's facilitator on a regular basis.

Regularly scheduled meetings with the facilitator will keep you up to date on the team's focus during meetings, how members are progressing in managing their meetings, and how effectively they are sharing leadership tasks. These factors are key in recognizing the team's readiness to move to the next level: the business-focus level.

4. Occasionally attend team meetings.

Make sure that you always let the team know in advance when you want to attend a team meeting so that they can put you on the agenda. You cannot expect the team to be serious about sticking to the agenda if you do not show respect for it as well. Also, be careful not to take over in meetings. Whenever you attend a meeting, have a brief huddle with the facilitator afterward to get feedback on how you came across in the meeting.

5. Step in when needed.

Sometimes the sponsor will need to step in and intervene when he or she sees the team going in the wrong direction. The table below lists some of the things you might see that require intervention and what you should do about them.

ACTIVITIES THAT REQUIRE REDIRECTION	WHAT THE SPONSOR DOES
Team is spending meeting time on issues outside its focus of control.	• Ensure that facilitator is at all meetings. • Have facilitator use the focus-of-control chart.
Team is working on issues that are difficult and long term in nature.	• Review team charter, stressing the performance factors. • Have facilitator take team through a problem-prioritizing session.
Team is not rotating responsibilities—one or two people are always taking on team tasks.	• Meet with team leader and facilitator to come up with a plan of action. • Build team activities into individual performance appraisals.

The t
ready
and s
levels
but cl
facilit
areas
their

This
the te
mem

We'll
follov
chan
and l
make
techr

ACTIVITIES THAT REQUIRE REDIRECTION	WHAT T
Team members do not understand team's purpose.	• Meet wi charter. • Ensure t stateme "buy in."
Team is trying to become a super problem-solving team rather than focusing on performance factors.	• Ensure f meetings • Offer to s to attack can refoc measure
Team is not meeting regularly.	• Meet with expectati members to meet.
Team is not using good processes in its meetings.	• Schedule meeting s • Ask facilit role. • Attend so

If yo
guid
of di

Ther
A lo
follov
prog

SECTION B: GROWING AND DEVELOPIN

Okay—you've given your team a proper start
structure is in place and members have receiv
guidance and direction. Now all you have to ∢
watch them grow, right? **WRONG!** You still h
to do. Developing a team is a lot like planting
after you have tilled the earth and sown the se
have work to do, ensuring that the garden is v
and fertilized. Although it is critical that you g
solid foundation to start with, helping the tean
important. Let's look at how you "grow" your

SPONSOR'S ROLE FOR THE LIFE OF THE TEAM

LEVEL-ONE ROLE	LEVEL-TWO ROLE	LEVEL-THREE ROLE	LEVEL-FOUR ROLE
Sponsor sets team's goals.	Team sets goals; sponsor approves and provides information to help set priorities.	Team sets goals; sponsor retains "veto" power.	Team sets goals; keeps sponsor informed of progress.
Sponsor makes sure that facilitator is at every meeting.	Team does not need facilitator at every meeting; sponsor ensures that the team has access to facilitator when needed.	Team rarely needs a facilitator. Exceptions may be situations of a heated issue or emotionally charged conflict.	Team has little to no need for a facilitator; need is more often in the area of technical advice or expertise.
Sponsor reviews team log frequently.	Sponsor reviews team logbook occasionally.	Sponsor rarely reviews logbook.	Sponsor does not review logbook.
	Sponsor keeps up with major projects and deadlines.	Sponsor keeps up with accomplishments in order to ensure publication.	Team takes responsibility for ensuring that successes are publicized.
Sponsor is the active "management" champion for the team.	Sponsor is the technical advisor and resource for the team.	Sponsor is training and information resource for the team.	Sponsor ensures that department budget will adequately fund the team's efforts; team administers budget.
Sponsor "directs" team activities according to the charter.	Sponsor "redirects" team's activities when members get off track.	Sponsor provides team with enough information to direct its own activities—still holds some "veto" power.	Team is "self-directing" based on both internal and external customer needs.

While the team is still at level one, your role will continue to be very strong. Below is a list of your specific level-one tasks.

➡	**Level-One Tasks**
➡	Set the team's goals.
➡	Review the team's performance measures.
➡	Approve the team's metrics.
➡	Sponsor any resulting ad hoc teams.
➡	Meet with facilitator or team leader on a regular basis.
➡	Publicize the team's successes.
➡	Redirect the team when they get off track.
➡	Monitor team meetings.
➡	Review the team logbook.

If you do your job well in structuring the team and then follow your task list, you should see signs that your team is mastering level one and is ready to move on to level two.

☞ Use this handy checklist to determine whether your team is ready to make the transition to level two.

LEVEL-ONE TEAM ADVANCEMENT CHECKLIST

✓	**ORGANIZATION**
❏	Team has a mission statement that all members understand and "buy in" to.
❏	Team has ground rules.
❏	Team keeps logbook up to date.
❏	Team meets on a regular basis.
✓	**MEETING PROCESS**
❏	Ground rules are observed and enforced.
❏	Meeting agendas are distributed prior to meeting.

(Continued)

✓	**MEETING PROCESS** (Concluded)
❏	Team uses round-robin.
❏	Team uses decision-making techniques that involve all members.
❏	Team uses action minutes during meeting and distributes them after meeting.
❏	Team uses parking lot effectively.
❏	Meeting roles are assigned and taken seriously.
❏	Team members are willing to lead a portion of a meeting or volunteer for tasks that must be completed between meetings.
❏	Team periodically evaluates its meetings.

✓	**TEAM DEVELOPMENT**
❏	Team is beginning to make own corrections in the team processes, relying less on the facilitator.
❏	Team members are able to confront and deal with some conflict, both in the meetings and in the workplace.
❏	All team members feel responsible for performance measures and the group focuses efforts on keeping those measures at an acceptable level.
❏	The team is able to solve minor problems that have a direct impact on its performance measures.
❏	Team members proactively seek input from internal customers before making changes to the work processes.
❏	Team listens to the input or feedback of others (e.g., sponsor, internal customer, facilitator) and responds appropriately.

You do not have to check off a magic number of activities before you can start helping the team move to level two. If you cannot check off a key area, then help the team get to the point where you can. When you see successes in most activities, give the team a boost to the next level.

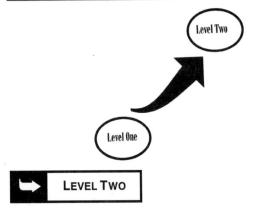

 LEVEL TWO

As a natural team advances to level two, its members become more business-oriented. They are not just working on how to get the job done, but also focusing on how to get it done better! They are becoming proactive—figuring out ways to meet future needs. When they see something in their process that needs changing, they act on it, gather data, and make their case to management. Whereas the level-one team does not act on a problem without someone's permission, the level-two team goes for it! Obviously the sponsor's role must change as the team becomes more active and results-oriented.

So what do you need to do once your team is operating at level two? You should continue to provide the team with direction and guidance, but at a lower level of intensity. The task list below is a good guide to follow.

	LEVEL-TWO TASKS

➡ Ensure that the team gains some problem-solving tools and techniques.

➡ Ensure that the team gains some data analysis and SPC tools and techniques.

LEVEL-TWO TASKS *(Concluded)*

➥ Ensure that the team receives advanced interpersonal skills training so members can begin dealing with some of their own communication and conflict issues rather than relying on facilitator.

➥ Ensure availability of facilitator while encouraging decreased reliance on facilitator.

➥ Provide information to the team about the department priorities and the facility vision.

➥ Provide financial information to the team (department budgets, operating cost figures, etc.).

➥ Initially provide enough information and guidance for the team to set its own goals.

➥ Empower the team to sponsor ad hoc teams in accomplishing goals.

➥ Teach the team, or have the facilitator teach the team, the necessary ingredients of the charter for ad hoc teams.

➥ Give the team a budget to administer for one of its ad hoc projects.

➥ Review the team's empowerment limits on decisions required to accomplish its jobs, looking for areas that can be expanded.

➥ Review team goals and give feedback as needed.

If you keep to the task list and modify your style as the team matures, you should see the team start to make progress toward level three. Then you will look for signs that the team is prepared to advance to the next level.

☞ Use the handy checklist on the following page to determine whether your team is ready to make the transition to level three.

LEVEL-TWO TEAM ADVANCEMENT CHECKLIST

✓	ORGANIZATION
❏	Team mission has a strong business purpose and focus.
❏	Team logbooks are maintained and updated by team members without reminders from facilitator.
❏	Team sponsors ad hoc teams to tackle major projects/problems—writing a charter and ensuring that the necessary support elements are in place.
❏	Task responsibilities are rotated on a regular basis.

✓	MEETING PROCESS
❏	Team meetings are managed without full-time facilitation.
❏	Team assertively enforces ground rules.
❏	Team members take feedback and input without defensiveness.
❏	Team uses decision-making techniques that involve all members.
❏	Team uses action minutes during meeting and distributes them after meeting.
❏	Team uses parking lot effectively.
❏	Team members participate fully and actively without coaching.
❏	Team evaluates its meetings and looks for ways to improve its process.

✓	TEAM DEVELOPMENT
❏	Team is using formal problem-solving tools and skills.
❏	Team is using SPC techniques.
❏	All team members focus on performance measures.
❏	The team is tackling more difficult problems that affect quality, productivity, or customer service measures.
❏	Team members proactively address problems.
❏	Team shows interest in continuing technical training.
❏	Team develops a total quality philosophy.
❏	Team actively seeks the input or feedback of customer (internal or external) and responds appropriately.

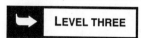

LEVEL THREE

Level-three activities may begin while the team is still operating at level two. Your job at this stage is to carefully plan and implement increased responsibilities for the team. The focus here differs from that of level one in these ways:

LEVEL-ONE FOCUS	→	LEVEL-THREE FOCUS
Sponsor looks at decisions that team members must be able to make in order to carry out their job duties.	→	Sponsor looks at areas that team members need to take responsibility for if they are to become self-managing.
Sponsor grants decision-making powers that probably should have been given to members earlier, before team was even started.	→	Sponsor looks at areas that traditionally have been supervisory in nature and draws up a plan for team to take on more of these areas.

The following list includes some of the areas in which you might begin to "release power" to the level-three team. Keep in mind that these are only examples; because every company has a different vision for its teams, some items may never become team responsibilities in your organization.

Human Resource Responsibilities

- Performance evaluations and appraisal
- Interviewing and making recommendations on new personnel
- Monitoring and keeping attendance records
- Discipline
- Conducting training and certification programs

Safety

- Conducting safety meetings and audits of own and other departments
- Designing and implementing safety programs

Production, Operations, Planning

- Making work assignments
- Production planning and scheduling
- Monitoring productivity and quality standards, recommending changes

Representing the Company

- Meeting with customers
- Dealing directly with customer complaints
- Auditing suppliers
- Meeting with vendors
- Certifying and approving vendors and suppliers

There are many ways that you can help your team assume increasing responsibility and thus advance to and master level three. The task list below is a useful reference.

 LEVEL-THREE TASKS

- Continue enhancing the team's problem-solving skills. Provide information and resources on advanced tools and techniques (cost benefit analysis, force field analysis, process capability, stratification).
- Get the team on the distribution list for publications, notices, and memos that previously came only to you.
- Increase the availability and level of financial information (e.g., department budgets, operating cost figures) afforded to the team.
- Arrange for team training in interviewing and hiring techniques (including legal issues, EEO issues, and so forth).
- Teach the team, or arrange for the human resources department to teach the team, about company policy on disciplinary actions, conducting performance counseling sessions, and documentation.

LEVEL-THREE TASKS *(Continued)*

➡ Increase the team's budgetary responsibilities. Give members a role in administering a part of whatever departmental budget the team has the greatest impact on.

➡ Encourage the team to appoint and rotate responsibility for traditional supervisory issues such as production, safety, and human resources. (The team may already rotate responsibility for reporting in these areas; however, each member's reporting role would now be expanded and include acting as the team leader whenever the team is dealing with an issue from the member's area.).

➡ Arrange for team training (formal or informal) in those areas in which members are increasing their decision-making roles.

➡ Smooth the way for the team to take over as a contact point for other functional areas by contacting the department head in the other areas.

➡ Call vendors/suppliers to let them know about the change in contact person to ensure an easy transition.

➡ Ensure that the team has a contact person for every functional area within the facility.

As you can see from the task list, you are still highly involved when sponsoring a level-three team. Your role is not an oversight or approval role, though. It has evolved into a **mentoring** role. You are trying to transfer to the team your knowledge and the knowledge of other staff professionals. This is **critical** because the team cannot advance to level four unless it is able to function **without you**. Thus your goal is to get members to the point where they know what you know. They must be able to get the information that you used to get for them, and they must know what to do with it!

It is also essential that members understand the team's weightier role in its areas of responsibility. When at level one or two, they may have been involved in those areas on an informal or input-only basis; but now, at level three, the areas are becoming part of the team's overall charge. Members are no longer simply accountable for their own performance factors and problem solving: they are getting into higher-level skills—the kind needed for the team to advance to level four.

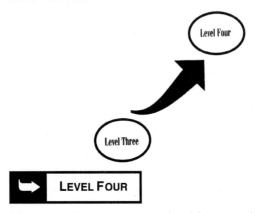

LEVEL FOUR

No remarkable gap separates a level-four team from a level-three team. Both teams have taken on traditional management or supervisory tasks. Yet there are some differences. The level-four team has little to no need for sponsor oversight, and—most important—while the level-three team may remain at the recommendation stage on certain issues, the level-four team is fully empowered to act on those issues.

To better see the differences between the two team types, let's compare several examples of team responsibilities. Don't forget—these are examples only. Your company may **not** intend to empower teams in these particular areas and have other areas in mind.

There is no task list for level four. You simply learn to increase the team's decision-making freedom, to step back as the team gains confidence and maturity. The transition is basically one of empowerment levels.

TEAM RESPONSIBILITIES	
LEVEL THREE	**LEVEL FOUR**
Interviewing internal candidates and making **recommendations** for new team members	Interviewing and **selecting** all candidates (both internal and external) for new team member positions
Giving input on evaluation and appraisal of other team member's performance	Evaluating and appraising each other's performance on the team Administering pay for performance plan according to company policy and guidelines
Selecting vendors based on predetermined criteria	Determining the criteria for selecting vendors Selecting vendors Negotiating with vendors
Communicating with vendors when there is a problem with quality, delivery, and the like	Communicating with vendors when there are problems Determining when it is necessary to stop doing business with a particular vendor because of continued problems
Determining training needs for the department; scheduling internal training for team members	Administering a training budget for the team Determining and scheduling internal and external training
Determining production schedules based on customer need (internal or external)	Determining production schedules based on customer need (internal or external) Determining manpower needs based on schedules
Ordering materials and dealing with suppliers	Managing a budget for materials and supplies
Giving input on production planning	Setting production plan according to customer needs
Actively monitoring productivity and quality standards	Setting and monitoring productivity and quality standards

You will find that the team needs less of your help as they transition into level four. If you do your job well, you will work your way out of a sponsorship role with this team. On occasion, team members may still turn to you for advice, for knowledge, for your special expertise. But, for the most part, they will be managing themselves and you will finally get to sit back and reap the rewards!

As a matter of fact, by the time this team reaches level four, you should have very little to do. So be prepared and work hard beforehand to find another role for yourself in the organization—maybe taking on some of your boss's former responsibilities. Or you can always start up another team . . .

 Congratulations!

After all your reading and hard work, it's time to find out how much of the information in this guidebook you've really absorbed.

The Team Sponsor Test begins on the next page. **Good luck!**

THE TEAM SPONSOR TEST

Directions: This test is a combination of multiple-choice, write-in, and true-or-false items. Closely read each item; then record your responses as appropriate. For multiple-choice questions, select only one answer. When you have completed the test, turn to Appendix B and check your responses to the test's answer key.

1. You have new equipment to install in the 213 area. Installation and testing will take at least two weeks. The equipment must be up and operational six weeks from today. You have decided to use a team for this task. Which type of team should you use?

   (a) The cross-shift natural team from the 213 area

   (b) A standing team chartered for this specific purpose

   (c) A cross-functional ad hoc team

   (d) A multi-functional engineering team

2. You have recently taken over as the sponsor of the Plant-Wide Quality Improvement Team. You find that the team does not have a charter or a mission statement and has not had a meeting in six months. The plant manager was the sponsor before your appointment. What should you do?

   (a) Go meet with the plant manager and review the team development guidelines with him, making sure he understands that teams must have structure.

   (b) Go to the teams coordinator and have a facilitator assigned, get help writing the charter, and meet with the team to make your expectations clear.

   (c) Call a team meeting to see what members think they should do to get on the right course.

   (d) Disband the team because members do not have the commitment necessary to carry out this task.

THE TEAM SPONSOR TEST *(Continued)*

3. You recently formed a natural team. You have met with the team, reviewed the charter, and asked members to write a mission statement. The mission statement they submitted to you for approval is as follows: *"Just Do It."*

   As the sponsor, what should you do?

   (a) Congratulate them for coming up with something brief, but share your concern that this seems to be a motto rather than a mission statement. Ask them to meet with their facilitator and work on a mission statement.

   (b) Let it go—after all, it's their team.

   (c) Go to the team leader, explain again what a mission statement is, and have the team leader handle it.

   (d) Meet with the team to let them know you're very disappointed in the way they have handled their first task and that you want them to do a better job on this.

4. You have a high-turnover area in which all the positions are entry level. Employees usually start out in this area and then bid out as soon as they get some experience. You want to accomplish some teaming in the area. What would be the best way?

   (a) A natural cross-shift team meeting once a month to work on inter-shift conflicts and communication

   (b) A natural customer team so that people will feel more committed to the jobs and not bid out

   (c) A standing team to work on long-term, critical issues for the area

   (d) Specific, short-term ad hoc teams as needed to improve the processes

THE TEAM SPONSOR TEST *(Continued)*

5. Which of the following elements is **not** necessary for an ad hoc team?

    (a) A charter

    (b) A sponsor

    (c) A mission statement

    (d) All of the above are necessary.

6. Which of the following goal statements is acceptable?

    (a) The team must complete this project as soon as possible.

    (b) The team must complete this project quickly.

    (c) The team must complete this project in a reasonable period.

    (d) None of the above is acceptable.

7. Which of the following statements is **not** true about the role of a standing team sponsor?

    (a) It is the sponsor's role to determine a standing team's metrics.

    (b) It is the sponsor's role to ensure that a standing team's goals will move the team toward its purpose.

    (c) It is the sponsor's role to set the boundaries for a standing team.

    (d) It is the sponsor's role to appoint the initial team leader.

8. Which of the following should you consider before you set up a standing team?

    (a) Whether or not the problem to be solved is a long-term, recurring issue.

    (b) Whether or not solving the problem will save money.

    (c) Whether or not the problem area has high turnover.

    (d) None of the above is a consideration in setting up a standing team.

THE TEAM SPONSOR TEST (Continued)

9. Your facility is experiencing problems with on-time deliveries. You think that the bottleneck is in the process that follows your group, but it is not in an area that you have control over. Which of the following actions should you take?

    (a) Set up a team in your area to handle your issues and let the manager of the other area worry about that area.

    (b) Go to the teams coordinator and explain the nature of the problem so that he can handle it.

    (c) Go to the manager of that area, share your thoughts on the problem, and offer to co-sponsor an ad hoc team made up of members from both areas.

    (d) Go to the plant manager and see if she has any interest in sponsoring a standing plant-wide team.

10. Several weeks ago, you chartered an ad hoc team to deal with some equipment problems that were a real issue in your department. The team solved the major problem: staying within the time frame that you set in the charter. However, members have continued to meet and work on the problem even though you formally disbanded them. They have achieved minor success, but you're fairly sure that they have achieved about all that they are going to. What should you do?

    (a) Make it very clear to members that you have disbanded the team and do not want them wasting any more time on issues that do not fit into your department's priorities.

    (b) Re-charter them even though you don't think they will have much success. You hate to "shoot them down" when they seem to be so motivated.

    (c) Ignore them. It won't hurt anything to let them meet, and they may even find a few more minor process improvements.

    (d) Meet with the team and ask them to submit a plan that outlines what they intend to work on, what the goal is, and how they are going to measure it, as well as a projected time frame. If you can support the plan they submit, you will re-charter the team. If not, you will explain why the team does not fit into the department priorities.

THE TEAM SPONSOR TEST *(Continued)*

11. In which of the following areas should a level-one natural team **not** be working?

    (a) Charting and tracking their performance measures

    (b) Improving their process

    (c) Interviewing and hiring new team members

    (d) Managing their meeting processes

12. Which of the following factors should you keep in mind as you structure a natural team?

    (a) Size of the area

    (b) How closely members work together

    (c) The business reason for forming a team

    (d) All of the above

13. At which team-development level (one, two, three, or four) should the sponsor ensure that the team has problem-solving skills?

    (a) Level one

    (b) Level two

    (c) Level three

    (d) Level four

14. What should the sponsor of a level-one natural team do if the team is not meeting on a regular basis?

    _____

    _____

15. Why is the natural team the most challenging team to sponsor?

    _____

    _____

THE TEAM SPONSOR TEST (Continued)

16. Name three of the four basic categories of performance
    measures for natural teams.

    _____

    _____

17. Who should write the natural team's mission statement?

    _____

18. There are six questions that you should ask in appointing the
    natural team leader. Write down any three of them.

    1. _____

    2. _____

    3. _____

19. The sponsor should write the natural team's operating guidelines

    ❏ True   ❏ False

    Justify your answer. _____

    _____

20. Name one of the ways that the sponsor monitors the
    development of the natural team.

    _____

21. The document that directs an ad hoc team toward goal
    accomplishment is the _____.

22. Which of the following should **not** be considered when selecting
    team members for an ad hoc team?

    (a) The number of other teams on which the person is serving

    (b) The type of experience the person has

    (c) The person's desire to solve the problem

    (d) All of the above should be considered.

THE TEAM SPONSOR TEST *(Continued)*

23. A person who has been trained in group processes and can help a team solve problems is a _____.

24. A _____ team is a type of team on which members sometimes rotate on and off the team.

25. Which of the following is **not** a good reason for disbanding an ad hoc team?

    (a) The team has achieved its goal.

    (b) The corporate office is moving the process the team is working on out of your plant.

    (c) After working with the team for three months, the facilitator tells you the team will not accomplish its goal.

    (d) The team leader quits.

26. The sponsor is not a member of the team and does not attend team meetings.

    ❏ True   ❏ False

27. Every ad hoc team must have a metrics planning table.

    ❏ True   ❏ False

28. The sponsor only intervenes when asked to by the facilitator.

    ❏ True   ❏ False

29. The sponsor ensures that team successes are documented and publicized.

    ❏ True   ❏ False

THE TEAM SPONSOR TEST *(Concluded)*

30. Which of the following issues would typically **not** be addressed by a standing team?

    (a)   Equipment installation

    (b)   Safety

    (c)   Supplier relationships

    (d)   Customer service

APPENDIX A

Team Charters

CONTENTS:

- Ad Hoc Team Charter
- Standing Team Charter
- Natural Team Charter

AD HOC TEAM CHARTER

Goal Statement *Identify causes of scrap on Line #2 and reduce it by 50%*

Team Sponsor: *Dan Jones*
Team Leader: *Bill Crittendon*
Assigned Facilitator: *Susan Lisle*
Time Frame: *3 Months*

Names of Team Members

Gail Williams
Lois Menendez
John Duncan
Will Brice

Boundaries

- *The team cannot change product specs*
- *The team cannot purchase new equipment without department head approval*

Budget/Resources *0*

May meet on overtime (1 hr. per wk.)
Maintenance – Mike Mays
Engineering – John Latimer

STANDING TEAM CHARTER

Team Purpose/Mission _The Safety & Environmental Team is to develop, administer, and constantly enhance all aspects of the Plant Safety program, and ensure communication to everyone in the facility_

Team Sponsor: _Chuck McClure_

Assigned Facilitator: _John Adams_

Team Members
Nadine Johnson (Team Leader)
Kent McCall
Judy Morris
Andy Danson
Susan Smith
John Williams

Boundaries
- May _not_ change existing safety policy without approval from Plant Mgr.
- May conduct audits in any dept.
- May require immediate change in safety practices if necessary

Budget/Resources
$10,000 for Safety Award Program

Word Processing Support from Plant Manager's office

NATURAL TEAM CHARTER

Team Name: _B-50 Team — Second Shift_

Team's Purpose: _Produce widgets that meet or exceed quality standards_

Team Job Description: _Team is responsible for preventative maintenance, housekeeping, supplying internal customers, and providing break coverage_

Team Sponsor: _John Lowe_

Team Leader: _John Jeffers_

Team Members: _Scott Sloan, Glenn Jenkins, Bernie Williams, Lisa Stone_

Decision-Making Authority
- Team may write work orders for routine maintenance & breakdowns
- Team will determine break schedules and vacation coverage
- Team will determine weekly meeting times

Boundaries
- Team must notify supervisor if repair will affect production schedule
- At least 2 team members must be in work area at all times
- Team may not meet more than one hour per week

APPENDIX B

Answer Keys

CHAPTER ONE

Practice Exercise—Three Cases

Case 1

1. Install and test new machinery beginning Monday at 7:00 a.m.

2. Successful installation will include a 24-hour testing and debugging period that must be complete by Wednesday at 11:00 p.m.

Case 2

1. Test all employee payroll records from the newly acquired plant and convert them to our personnel system by the February payroll.

2. February payroll is successfully completed with 95% accuracy. No more than 5% of the paychecks for the new employees are handwritten.

Case 3

1. Determine the root cause of the increased scratched widgets. Determine best course of action to reduce the number of scratched widgets.

2. The crew's rate of rejects due to scratched widgets should be reduced by 50% within 30 days.

Exercise—Evaluating Metrics

Situation A

No. The metric will measure only the number of team members who have completed the training. It tells you nothing about the proficiency level they have achieved. The team should consider changing the metric to "track the number of maintenance team members who complete the eight-hour training in problem-solving techniques and pass the proficiency test by April 15."

Situation B

Yes. The team must develop a baseline of top pad scrap in order to set a level of improvement. Charting the data by the hour may also give them some clue as to where problems lie.

CHAPTER TWO

Exercise—Reviewing Short-Term Goals

Short-Term Goal 1

1. Yes. Awareness and understanding on the part of individual employees will certainly help send the message that quality is an issue that all employees must take responsibility for.

2. No. The metric will simply measure the number of people who have received the training. The goal statement is to ensure understanding.

Short-Term Goal 2

1. Yes. The assumption is that if operators are following the standard operating procedures, problems in the processes are less likely.

2. Yes. The audit will give a good indication of the use and knowledge of SOPs. Auditors should also ensure that operators receive feedback where needed.

CHAPTER THREE

Exercise—Performance Measures

Situation A

1. The teams' measures are volume; therefore, to meet their volume requirements, they are concentrating on the work that can be done the fastest. The teams are giving management what it is asking for—large numbers of items. But the customer is asking for timely deposit.

2. The teams' measures should focus on the time that lapses between arrival in the office and deposit. If they concentrate on getting the items processed as quickly as possible, the volume will follow.

Situation B

1. The measures allow this team to gauge whether they are living up to their mission. Both measures tell the team whether they are meeting their on-time, every-time goal.

2. The team needs to add a measure of the number or percentage of parts rejected by the internal customer. They have no measures to tell them if they have met their second goal: "One hundred percent of parts delivered will meet customer requirements." It may be helpful to chart the number of parts rejected, as well as the reason for rejection.

THE TEAM SPONSOR TEST ANSWERS

1. C
2. B
3. A
4. D
5. C
6. D
7. A
8. A
9. C
10. D
11. C
12. D
13. B

14. Meet to clarify expectations and have the team pick a regular meeting time

15. Because it is not a voluntary team, everyone in the area must participate whether interested or not.

16. Quality, quantity, timeliness, cost

17. The team

18. Is this someone whom the team members look up to and respect? Who does his or her share of the work willingly? Who is willing to seek help when needed? Who is well organized and a good communicator? Who will be strong enough to refocus the team if members stray into inappropriate areas? Who can coordinate and lead without becoming a "mini-supervisor"?

19. False. The operating guidelines lay out how the team will get work done—team members must feel committed to the plan.

20. Has team track and report performance measures; reviews logbook; meets with facilitator; occasionally attends meetings; steps in when needed.

21. Charter

22. D

23. Facilitator

24. Standing

25. D

26. True

27. False

28. False

29. True

30. A

APPENDIX C

Sponsor Extras

CONTENTS:

- Metrics Planning Table
- Action Minutes Form
- Meeting Agenda Form
- Parking Lot Form
- Sample Team Mission Statement
- Sample Ground Rules
- Sample Operating Guidelines

METRICS PLANNING TABLE

Team Name: _Line 2 Team_   Team Sponsor: _Dan Jones_

Goal: _Identify causes of scrap on Line #2 and reduce it by 50%_

	Measurement 1	Measurement 2	Measurement 3	Measurement 4
What will be measured?	% of Scrap			
How will it be measured?	Scrap will be counted & recorded hourly			
Team member responsible for measurement	Machine operator			
How long will it be measured?	4 weeks			
What will be considered a successful solution?	50% reduction			

Action Minutes

Note: One of three things must happen: Items must (1) be resolved, or (2) placed on the parking lot form, or (3) entered on this action plan.

ACTION ITEM	ASSIGNED TO	TARGET DATE FOR COMPLETION	STATUS

Meeting Agenda

Meeting Date/Time _____ Location _____

Purpose of the Meeting:

Background Information:

Please Bring:

AGENDA ITEM	PERSON RESPONSIBLE	PROCESS	TIME

Parking Lot

Note: One of three things must happen: Items must (1) be resolved, or (2) placed on this parking lot form, or (3) assigned to someone as an action step.

Parking Lot

ITEM #		REMARKS
1.		
2.		
3.		
4.		
5.		
6.		
7.		

TEAM MISSION STATEMENT

Who we are and what we do:

The B-52 team exists to:

- Produce the highest quality widgets as efficiently as possible
- Solve problems in our process quickly and effectively, with input from all team members
- Always look for better and more efficient ways of producing our product

We will accomplish these goals by valuing each other's opinions, treating each other with respect, and developing a supportive work environment.

Signatures of Team Members:

GROUND RULES
B-52 TEAM - FIRST SHIFT

1. We will be respectful of others on the team.

2. We will be patient and understanding with each other.

3. We will be flexible.

4. We will be considerate of each other.

5. We will be honest and tactful.

6. We will be dedicated and on time (to work and to meetings).

7. We will be open to suggestions from others.

8. We will stay focused and on task in our meetings and in our workplace.

OPERATING GUIDELINES FOR B-52 TEAM — DAY SHIFT

B-52 TEAM	TEAM INFORMATION	COMMENTS
Meeting Dates and Times	Tuesdays at 2:30 p.m.	
Meeting Location	Team meeting room	
Agendas to be posted — when and where:	Cafeteria bulletin board by Friday a.m.	
Action Minutes distributed to:	Department Superintendent/ Facilitator	
Team Sponsor	Melinda Farmer	581-1525
Meeting Facilitator	Jean Johnson	
Supplies/Purchasing	John Hughes	588-7912
Maintenance	John Smithberger	588-7072/588-8052
Engineering	Leo Landan	588-8662
Training	Anne Henson	230-5229

APPENDIX D

Problems & Solutions Index

CONTENTS:

- 20 Most Frequent Team Sponsorship Problems and Solutions

PROBLEMS & SOLUTIONS INDEX

1. The team I'm sponsoring is spending all its time
    generating lists of things that other groups need to do—
    Engineering, Maintenance, Management, other shifts, etc.
    What can I do to focus team members on what they need
    to do?

    *Your first step is to re-evaluate this team's charter. You must
    ensure that the team has something substantive to focus efforts
    on and that you have granted clear authority to act on those
    substantive issues. If there is any chance that the charter is not
    clear, schedule a meeting to clarify your expectations along with
    the empowerment limits.*

    *If you are certain that the problem is not with the charter, ask the
    facilitator to take the team through a focus of control exercise. In
    this exercise, the facilitator puts three columns on a flipchart.
    The first column is labeled "Under Team Control," the second
    column is labeled "Under Team Influence," and the final column
    is "No Control." The facilitator has the team plot each of the
    ideas/solutions/issues in the appropriate column. This visual
    chart allows the team members to see that they are spending a lot
    of time on things that they can do little to nothing about. The
    facilitator can then lead a discussion on how the team can begin
    to focus on the areas in the first column, those "under team
    control."*

2. I'm having trouble coming up with boundaries for my
    team. What kinds of things are usually in the boundaries
    and why do I have to have them?

    *Boundaries often pose the greatest challenge in constructing the
    charter. It can be difficult to think of all the things that the team
    can and cannot do. However, boundaries are critical to the
    success of the team. The pitfalls of a team without boundaries
    vary based on the culture of your organization. If employees*

have always felt very limited in empowerment issues, the team may develop self-imposed boundaries that are more restrictive than you intend. Members may feel a sense of powerlessness that leads to the "list-making" activities we talked about in question #1. On the other hand, some employees take the lack of boundaries to mean that anything is "fair game." Once they get started on issues that are outside the boundaries, it becomes very difficult to rein them back in without impacting their motivation. Setting up the boundaries after members have stepped out of them leads to resentment, anger, and distrust in the team process.

Developing boundaries is simply a matter of taking the time to think through what you cannot accept as the sponsor. If there are solutions, ideas, or actions that you simply cannot live with, those must be included in the boundaries. If there are laws, policies, or guidelines that limit the team, those must be included or referred to in the boundaries. There may be personnel policies, work rules, or other internal guidelines that the team must be aware of in the boundaries. Other ideas for brainstorming boundaries might include schedules, product specifications, service delivery levels, vendor contracts, material requirements, or quality levels. One critical point to remember in writing the boundaries is to include "can's" along with the "cannot's."

3. It seems like it takes a lot of time to sponsor a team. How much time will I have to devote to this process of sponsoring a team?

   Most of the time invested in sponsoring a team is on the front-end. It does take some time to write a charter and you should meet with the team initially to gain agreement to the charter. You will probably find that the team needs more guidance and direction in the beginning and then begins to require less from you as it proceeds with the project or mission.

4. I have natural teams that I'm sponsoring in my area, along with several ad hoc teams. I'm having a hard time paying attention to all of them. How many teams can I realistically support?

Unfortunately, the answer to this question depends on a couple of factors. The availability of facilitators and the level of team maturity are critical factors in determining how many teams one sponsor can support. If there are skilled facilitators available for every team and if the employees have participated in decision-making activities in the past, you may be able to support several teams (possibly up to eight). However, if the team members are new to the concept, if there has been minimal team training, or if the facilitators are weak, you should probably limit your sponsorship to two or three teams.

5. I've sponsored several ad hoc teams that did a great job and saved the company a lot of money and time. Our company does not pay bonuses for these kinds of activities. Are there other ways I can reward these teams?

   This is an issue that many sponsors have to deal with. Very few compensation programs incorporate teams or team activities. If you have no way to compensate team members monetarily, there are several other meaningful options.

   ✓ *Personal letters thanking team members for their efforts*

   ✓ *Corporate recognition such as letters or articles in corporate-wide newsletters*

   ✓ *Company bulletin board that announces and touts team accomplishments*

   ✓ *Appreciation days or dinners for team members*

   In addition to these ideas, you may be able to use the employee performance appraisal system to recognize team activities.

   The recognition does not have to cost money. However, you should avoid things like hats, t-shirts, or other small tokens. For some reason, those don't seem to sit well with many team members, possibly because the cost per unit sends a conflicting message about the value of their contribution.

6. Since the sponsor is not supposed to attend the team's meetings, how can I know whether the team is performing effectively?

There are several options for keeping up with your team's activities. If you have specific reports that you want from the team, make that clear in the charter. If your team is working on a project that has critical milestones, ask them to meet with you at each of those milestones to keep you in the loop.

You may also have the team keep a logbook of team activities. The logbook should have the charter, the team's operating guidelines, agendas for each meeting, followed by the action minutes and parking lot forms from those meetings. If the team is using our suggested form for minutes, it will only take one glance to see what type of actions the team is taking, whether assignments are balanced among team members, and the status of each. The status column is critical in identifying the barriers that have stymied the team's efforts.

Meetings with the team leader or the facilitator are also helpful in keeping up with your team's progress and give you a chance to find out how you can support the team's efforts.

7. I am sponsoring a team whose team leader is the most ineffective member. I allowed the team to pick their own leader but now I wish I had not. What can I do?

The team is going to have a tough time meeting goals with an ineffective leader. Your first step is to ensure that you have provided the team leader with the training and role clarification he or she needs to be successful. Find out what your organization offers in team leader training and make sure that this team leader participates in all available training. You or the facilitator must also coach the leader on the skills needed for successful team leadership. Make your expectations clear by developing a written job description and possibly building these skills into the performance appraisal. Finally, you may have to ask the facilitator to play a very active role with this team.

Do not simply remove the team leader from the role without doing everything possible to provide the skills necessary for success. Team members need to see that the organization is going to help all employees in the transition to a team environment.

8. I have sponsored a team to work on issues that require support from another area and it is not getting that support. I have spoken with the department head of that area and he assured me that he would follow up on things, but nothing has changed. What do I do next?

    This problem seems to be a result of team structure. Whenever you sponsor a team that is going to overlap areas, it should include customers and suppliers. Correcting the team composition is the quickest fix for this problem. You should re-charter this team, co-sponsoring it with this other manager. The team should be made up of employees from both areas and must be structured in such a way that solving the problem(s) benefits both areas.

9. I have 50 people in one area that all perform the same job on three different shifts. How can I configure teams that fit the rule of "small in size"?

    This is a common problem. You may be able to structure small focused teams by subgrouping members around product, customer, process, or some other factor. If not, you may find that your best means of accomplishing teams and team work is through standing teams. Standing teams can be set up around very specific drivers such as cost, quality, safety, housekeeping. The membership rotates with representation from each shift and each job responsibility. The standing team spins off ad hoc teams as needed to solve problems and address issues. For more information on setting up effective standing teams, see Chapter 2.

10. When I go to team meetings and try to get involved in the team's activities to show my support, team members seem to resent it. I don't want the team to think I'm uninterested in its activities by stepping back too far. How do I find a balance?

You should attend team meetings:

- *At the team's inception*

- *Whenever invited*

- *At any critical milestone in a team project*

- *Any time that the team has a crisis or support issues requiring your intervention*

Remember—you turned the "how-to's" over to the team members. If you come to team meetings any more often than the above list, they will feel that you don't trust them to come up with the right answers.

11. If I have formed a team to solve a specific problem, who makes the final decision on the solution, me or the team?

Once again the answer to this question goes back to the charter. A well written charter specifically states the team's decision-making authority. However, be very careful that you don't have a certain solution or answer in mind before you sponsor the team. Often managers believe they already have the best answer but they start a team in order to gain "buy-in." This approach rarely works—team members have their own ideas about how to deal with an issue and it's usually different than what you had in mind. If you have already decided how you want a problem solved, make it clear in the charter that this team is an implementation or recommendation team. However, try to avoid these types of teams unless you truly believe that there is only one right way to address an issue. Whenever you can empower employees to make decisions, you send strong messages about your trust in their abilities. And so long as you write a charter that clearly states the boundaries, empowerment is actually easier. Coming up with the right answer to everyone else's problems is no longer your job. Supporting others in coming up with the answers is a much more important role for today's manager.

12. One of my best employees is constantly being asked to serve on teams throughout the organization. I don't want to limit her opportunities but I also don't want to see her "burn-out" on teams. How many teams should a person serve on?

   Good question! Often the best team players are rewarded with more work. A good rule of thumb is no more than two project teams in addition to membership on the natural team. However, it is important to look at this number case by case, and team member by team member. Some teams have a long time frame or require minimal involvement, others can become a full-time job in their own right. Some employees thrive on a variety of activities, while others prefer to focus on one issue at a time and gain closure. Look at each situation separately and sit down with the employee involved to talk through what is required with each team, along with other job obligations.

13. If I have a team that is "off-track" and working on issues outside the charter, how do I step in without squelching team members' motivation?

   Feedback is critical—and it should occur as quickly as possible, before the team gets too far off track. You should schedule a meeting with the team to review the charter and provide additional information if the charter is not clear. During this meeting, you must be able to describe clearly how and why the actions are outside the scope of the team. You should also be prepared to make suggestions about some things that the team could focus on that are within the parameters. Be sure that the team is actually outside the boundaries and not simply pursuing a course different than your preferred course of action. Remember, you decided to turn this over to the team!

14. Whenever I ask people to volunteer for teams, I get the same people over and over. Should I appoint team members in order to get more involvement from others?

If you are continually getting the same volunteers for team activities, you run the risk of burning out your best team players. By all means, appoint team members for your next team. Sit down with the team leader or facilitator and decide on appointees based on aptitude for solving the problem, experience with the problem, time available to work on the problem, or diversity of thought processes or approaches. Once you have decided who you will ask to serve on the team, meet with the appointees individually and explain why they have been asked to serve on the team and gain their commitment to the project.

15. I don't think the natural teams in my area are holding effective meetings. The minutes indicate that they are using meeting time for information sharing only. How do I intervene?

You are right to be concerned about this problem. The information dissemination meeting is guaranteed to produce boredom, while wasting valuable work time. When teams get caught up in these types of meetings they wind up with little sense of accomplishment. Your first step should be to work with the facilitator. If the team does not have a facilitator at every meeting, then immediately have one assigned. The facilitator must ensure that the team develops action-oriented agendas for every meeting. Every meeting should have an overall purpose statement and a couple of objectives that contain action verbs, along with expected outcomes. The facilitator should help the team leader develop and distribute the agenda prior to the meeting so that the members come to the meeting prepared to make decisions and take actions.

16. When team members have conflicts or problems, they won't deal directly with each other. Instead they come to me to intervene. What should I do?

Bad news—if you have been intervening every time the team members come to you, you have taught them that this is the way to handle conflict. Your first and most difficult step is to undo that message. The team must meet and talk about conflicts and how it wants to handle them. Team members should work with their facilitator to identify the processes and procedures that they can all agree to use when one-on-one or team conflicts occur. This discussion must take place when there is no conflict going on. Once the process has been agreed on, you must help them follow through with using it. Each time that the team members come to you to with a conflict (and they will continue to come to you at first), you must ask them if they have followed the process and direct them back to it. Make it clear that you will not intervene until the team has exhausted all options within the agreed on process, then stick to your word, no matter how much you might like to step in.

17. The teams that I have chartered have not come up with solutions that are reasonable or feasible. What am I doing wrong?

    This is beginning to sound like a broken record—but you must go back to your charters. If your teams have not come up with feasible solutions, you haven't done a good job with the boundaries or the goal statements. If you take the time on the front end to write a good charter, you will save countless hours in wasted efforts. Compare the charters you've developed to the charters of other teams in your organization that you consider successful. You may be able to pick up ideas from these charters. The team coordinator may also be able to help you analyze and improve your existing charters. Also, you should meet with any teams that you sponsor after they've had a chance to review and react to the charter. Sometimes there are misunderstandings with even the best charters. Nothing can replace the face-to-face interaction that a meeting can provide, allowing members to ask questions and clarify understanding.

    You must also make sure that you are following the recommendations for question 5. If you're not finding out until the end of the team project that the team is off-base, you haven't followed team activities closely enough. Check-in meetings at major milestones can head off a big surprise at the end of the

*project. Reviewing the team logbook will also help keep you in
the loop so that you do not find yourself disappointed with the
end results.*

*The facilitator may also be able to help ensure your future teams
are more successful. If the teams are truly not making good
decisions, they may need more guidance in the use of tools to
analyze problems, identify causes, and evaluate solutions. The
fairly simple mechanics of good problem-solving techniques can
make the difference between success and failure for any team.
Ensuring that the team receives appropriate training and
utilizing a skilled facilitator will go a long way toward helping
you get the results-orientation you want from your teams.*

18. I chartered a team for one purpose but now a change in
    corporate direction dictates that this team change course as
    well. How do I communicate that to the team and
    minimize the resentment that is likely to occur?

    *Your course of action depends on how dramatic the change in
    direction will be for the team. If the change is radical, you are
    probably better off disbanding the team after explaining the
    reasons and thanking the members for their time. You can then
    re-charter another team with the new direction in mind. The
    membership may remain the same or the change may also dictate
    some difference in make-up.*

    *On the other hand, if the change is such that you believe you can
    make minor adjustments in the charter and proceed, then make
    those changes in writing, give them to the team, and schedule a
    meeting for questions and clarification. If necessary, gather more
    information about the change in corporate direction so that you
    are prepared to answer their questions about the overall change,
    as well as the change for the team. Share as much information
    with team members as possible.*

19. I don't like the solution that one of my ad hoc teams has
    come up with. How do I communicate my dissatisfaction
    and get members to go back to the drawing board?

First, you must take a hard look at your reaction. Why don't you like the team's solution? Is it outside the parameters of the charter? Does it not address the issue? If your problem with the solution is simply that it is not the solution you would have chosen had you been solving the problem, you are making a big mistake to reject it. If the team stayed within the parameters and has come up with a solution or answer that the entire team supports, you are going to have a hard time justifying rejection. That action will send the message that you had a specific answer in mind and that the team just didn't come up with it. This is a sure, quick way to turn these members off to teams. However, if you truly have some legitimate concerns about the effectiveness of the solution, don't disband the team yet. Have members implement a pilot, gather data, and analyze the results. Then if they end up going back to the drawing board, it's not you that sent them there, it's the data.

20. I don't have time to write charters for all the teams I have. Why can't I just get the team leader or facilitator to write the charter?

Writing a good charter does take time. You may want to describe your vision for the team to the facilitator or team leader. She or he may then develop a rough draft of the charter. You must review the draft, carefully examining the boundaries, goals, and focus. Make any necessary changes and submit the draft charter to the team. Don't forget that team members need to review the charter and make suggested revisions at their first meeting. It's a good idea to meet with the team either during this first meeting or afterwards to gain agreement to the charter.

APPENDIX E

Sponsor's Guide to Team Recognition

SPONSOR'S GUIDE TO TEAM RECOGNITION

As teams and team members contribute to the success of a business, those contributions should be recognized and rewarded. However, rewards can be tricky, especially monetary rewards. If an organization's goal is for their employees to feel that continuous improvement is part of their everyday job, rewarding team activities may send a conflicting message. It may say to employees that working on a team is not part of the job, rather that it is above and beyond the call of duty. On the other hand, if profits grow and the company becomes more competitive because of team efforts, team members may feel exploited and angry if that gain is not shared. Therefore, changes in the compensation and bonus system should be carefully thought through and carried out only after in-depth study and help from compensation experts.

Where does that leave the individual sponsor who wants to recognize successful teams? Despite the chilling warning about the complexities of team compensation, the innovative sponsor can still find creative ways to recognize the contributions of teams. To be effective, these "rewards" must be a sincere expression of appreciation on the part of the sponsor. Trinkets and small dollar items do more harm than good if they are not accompanied by a genuine, personal "thank you."

It is fairly easy to know when and how to recognize ad hoc teams, since they have a very specific goal to reach and a time frame in which to do it. Standing and natural teams are a little more difficult to recognize because their goals are longer term. Therefore, the team's intermediate goals and measures become extremely important. If a sponsor is to be effective in recognizing results and keeping the momentum going for long term teams, it is critical that he or she keeps abreast of the intermediate goals and results.

Ideas for recognition

✓ "Bragboards" where all team accomplishments are posted for the rest of the organization to see.

Not only will the bragboard serve the purpose of recognizing the team, it will also communicate to others how teams are impacting the organization.

✓ Team of the Month reserved parking spaces.

Since many organizations have eliminated reserved spaces, a month without fighting for a parking space may be much appreciated. If parking is not a big deal at your facility, perhaps free coffee for the month is another idea. Look for something that continues to remind the team of your appreciation after the project is complete.

✓ A catered meal with the team as guests of honor.

A catered meal or going out for a meal with the sponsor can be a highly effective means of recognizing the team. Of course, it is critical that the meal is combined with a sincere expression of appreciation from the sponsor.

✓ A public thank you to the team during an organization-wide meeting.

Most organizations have monthly or quarterly communication meetings. Whether it is department-wide or across the entire organization, public praise is highly effective in recognizing a team's accomplishments. The sponsor must ensure that the praise specifically mentions the team's results, citing numbers and/or dollars when possible.

✓ **Personal "thank you" letters to each member of the team, with a copy to the personnel file.**

It is critical that the letter be personal and specific. The sponsor must detail the team's impact on the organization and, if possible, each member's contribution. It is very important that it not come across as a form letter. A handwritten note may be as effective as a formal letter.

✓ **Establish a club in your organization, such as the Million Dollar Club, and induct teams who save the company significant amounts of money.**

Teams often make significant contributions to the bottom-line in organizations. Establishing a club or hall-of-fame for those who have saved the company money, increased production, or improved customer service can be an effective means of recognition.

✓ **Invite teams who make significant strides to present their success at a management team meeting.**

Teams like to know that they are getting credit for their ideas, rather than simply making someone else look good. Inviting the team to present their stories at a management staff meeting assures them that you are "sharing the glory."

✓ **Host a field day for the team.**

The event could be bowling, an amusement park, the movies, a museum or local attraction. Any kind of activity that allows the team to have fun together after working through a tough project not only shows appreciation, it may also build even more teamwork between the members.

✓ **Gift certificates for each member of the team to take his or her spouse out to a nice meal at a local restaurant.**

This particular reward includes the spouse of the team members and is very appropriate when a project has taken up a good deal of energy and time, since it shows appreciation for the patience and support of the spouse.

✓ **Spotlight in the organization's internal newsletter or communications piece highlighting the team's accomplishments.**

Like the bragboard, this particular mechanism for recognition allows the sponsor to ensure that others in the organization know about the project and highlights the value of teams in the organization, hopefully helping to draw in more participation.

✓ **A day in which the sponsor agrees to be the team's "gopher" by running errands or helping the team members out with the annoying details of their daily jobs.**

Everyone likes to see that the boss is willing to get his or her hands dirty sometimes. Taking a day out of your schedule to do some of the less pleasant aspects of your team members' jobs can go a long way toward showing appreciation, and may even give you a new appreciation for some of the things you didn't know about others' jobs.

✓ **Plaques or certificates presented to the team by the sponsor and/or the sponsor's boss.**

Bringing in your boss may help reinforce how valued the team's contribution is. However, remember that the genuine verbal expression of appreciation is just as important as the plaque or certificate itself.

For more ideas on innovative approaches to recognition, *1001 Ways to Reward Employees* by Bob Nelson, Workman Publishing offers simple methods for recognizing employee contributions. Remember, whatever method you select has to be accompanied by a sincere sense of appreciation for how these team members have helped the organization.

ABOUT THE AUTHOR

Sara Pope is a senior associate with Cornelius and Associates, an international consulting firm headquartered in Columbia, South Carolina. She provides custom training and consulting help to clients in maximizing the performance of employees and work teams. Ms. Pope has worked in both manufacturing and service industries, helping clients to focus on the right things, maintain the discipline to follow effective improvement processes, develop high performing people and work teams, and achieve startling business results.

To receive more information about Ms. Pope's other workbooks and resources, or to find out how to schedule a training session on team sponsorship or related topics, please contact:

Cornelius and Associates
631-G Harden Street
Columbia, SC 29205
803-779-3354
803-254-0183 (Fax)